Resolving Conflicts
How to Get Along When You Don't Get Along

ISSUES IN FOCUS TODAY

Karen Judson

 Enslow Publishers, Inc.

40 Industrial Road   PO Box 38
Box 398   Aldershot
Berkeley Heights, NJ 07922   Hants GU12 6BP
USA   UK

http://www.enslow.com

Library of Congress Cataloging-in-Publication Data

Judson, Karen, 1941-
    Resolving conflicts : how to get along when you don't get along / Karen Judson.
        p. cm. — (Issues in focus today)
    Includes bibliographical references and index.
    ISBN 0-7660-2359-1
    1. Conflict management—Juvenile literature. I. Title. II. Series.
    HM1126.J83 2005
    303.6'9—dc22

                                                        2004028119

Printed in the United States of America

10 9 8 7 6 5 4 3 2 1

To Our Readers:
We have done our best to make sure all Internet Addresses in this book were active and
appropriate when we went to press. However, the author and the publisher have no control
over and assume no liability for the material available on those Internet sites or on other
Web sites they may link to. Any comments or suggestions can be sent by e-mail to com-
ments@enslow.com or to the address on the back cover.

Illustration Credits: AP/Wide World, pp. 22, 33, 67; BananaStock, pp. 1, 3, 36, 49, 56, 90;
Corel Corp., p. 12, EyeWire Images, pp. 3, 46, 75; Digital Vision, pp. 3, 9, 94; Hemera
Image Express, pp. 43, 70, 99; Library of Congress, p. 63; Photos.com, pp. 3, 17, 26, 38,
51, 81, 83, 103, 105.

Cover Illustration: Photos.com (photo); Corel Corp. (background).

C o n t e n t s

Author's Note

Some of the names in this book are fictional,
but the stories come out of the author's own experience
as a parent and teacher. All of the words, feelings, and
situations described are based on real people's
experiences with conflict and conflict resolution.

What Is Conflict?

How can conflict be defined? Imagine the following scenarios:

- You just found out that one of your friends is dating the guy who just broke up with you, and you feel betrayed by both your friend and your ex-boyfriend.

- Your parents refuse to let you go camping with a group of your friends because the group consists of both boys and girls, and you are angry because you think that your parents do not trust you.

- It is frustrating that even though you have just earned your driver's license, your father will not let you take the car by yourself.

- You have been looking forward to the prom for months, but now it is only two weeks away and your boss will not give you time off.

- A customer where you work blames you—unjustly but loudly—for shortchanging her.

- For the third time this month your girlfriend stands you up.

- You got a ticket for speeding that you feel you did not deserve, but when you tried to talk the police officer out of it, he got angry.

- A friend invited you to see a movie, but you lied and said your parents would not let you go. The truth was that you thought someone you had a crush on was going to ask you to the same movie, and you wanted to be free to accept that invitation. The person you lied to now seems to dislike you, and you feel guilty.

Do these situations sound familiar? They're called conflicts, and they are a part of daily life. Sometimes you may think you have more than your share, but you are not alone. Everyone experiences conflict—from the president of the United States (of course, his job is handling conflicts) to kids in kindergarten (remember when you and another five-year-old fought furiously over the crayon you both wanted?).

Conflicts can arise as we interact with strangers, family members, employers, authority figures, acquaintances, friends, members of groups we belong to, and others. Maybe you want to ride the roller coaster at an amusement park and the attendant says you do not meet the height requirement. Perhaps you believe the low grade you received on a test was in error. Maybe you and your parents do not agree on your choice of friends. Or perhaps the basketball team you play on cannot agree on which player to elect team captain. Some conflicts cause a stronger emotional response than others. It would probably be more difficult, for example, to resolve a conflict with your parents over your choice of friends than to decide which teammate to elect captain.

We tend to think of any kind of conflict as hurtful, but a personal conflict is not always wrong and does not always involve an angry confrontation. A life totally without conflict might sound desirable, but it would most likely become boring. Life is interesting because it is filled with surprises, expectations, disappointment—and conflict. On the other hand, sometimes conflicts lead to hostility and worse, and if not resolved they can make life miserable for everyone involved.

There is no doubt that conflict creates challenges, but conflict does not mean that a fight is unavoidable or that the individuals involved in a conflict will become enemies. The key to successfully meeting challenges and growing in the process is learning how to handle conflict. Consider the following example:

> **A life totally without conflict might sound desirable, but it would most likely become boring. Life is interesting because it is filled with surprises, expectations, disappointment—and conflict.**

Fourteen-year-old Brian and his twelve-year-old sister, Emily, live on a 20-acre ranch outside Denver, Colorado. When they recently moved out of the city to the ranch, they each wanted a horse, but their parents told them that they would have to help buy the horses themselves. Their parents would pay for hay, veterinary bills, and tack, but the two siblings would have to pay at least half of the purchase price for the horses. Brian and Emily pooled their savings but could not manage even half of the price of two saddle horses. "We have enough money for one horse, so let's buy one horse together," Emily suggested, "and we'll both ride it."

"Good idea," Brian agreed. "We'll save our allowances and any money we earn until we have enough for a second horse."

The plan sounded workable, and the two bought a horse they both liked. The one thing Brian and Emily had not anticipated, however, was the conflict that arose when both co-owners wanted to ride the horse at the same time. For instance, Emily had a slumber party and her three guests wanted to ride Beau, the new gelding. But that same evening, Brian brought four friends home after school and they, too, were eager to ride the new horse.

Emily was the first to capture the horse, and she helped one of her friends mount before Brian could intervene.

"You're such a brat, Emily," Brian shouted. "By the time you and your friends finish, it will be too late for me and my friends."

"I'm telling Mom you called me a brat." Emily stormed into the house with her friends in tow.

A compromise was arranged, in which each of Brian's friends would alternate with each of Emily's friends for a twenty-minute ride. No one was entirely satisfied with the arrangement, however. The rides were too short, Brian and Emily continued to argue, and the horse was nervous over the frequent changes in riders and nearly dislodged a couple of his passengers. It was apparent after all the guests went home that some sort of structured, mutually acceptable arrangement would be necessary if the horse co-ownership was to work.

Clearly, Brian and Emily were in the middle of a conflict that would have to be resolved before they could enjoy their shared horse.

What Is Conflict?

The dictionary defines *conflict* as:

- Fight; battle
- Competitive or opposing action
- Antagonistic state or action
- Mental struggle

Conflicts are clashes—disagreements—between or among individuals, members of a group, or nations. (When nations fail at conflict resolution, wars or military actions can result.) Conflicts can also be internal—occurring within yourself. This can happen for many reasons, such as when you feel torn between your feelings and what you or others see as the "right" behavior in a situation, as the example mentioned in the chapter opening, where a person lies to a friend then feels guilty. Internal conflicts often arise when you need to make a decision and you cannot decide. Your mother chooses your clothes for you, but she doesn't know what's cool. You wish she would stop, but if you tell her she will be hurt and angry. Three of the

Conflict can start over issues as minor as who has the red crayon.

colleges you apply to have accepted you, and now you have to decide which one to attend.

Every individual has beliefs, values, goals, behavior patterns, needs, wants, interests, and opinions that are unique to that individual. The individuals that make up a nation have collective customs, habits, and religious and political views, as well, that make them distinct from people in other nations. It is not surprising, therefore, that when individuals or nations interact, these unique characteristics sometimes collide, or that when individuals act contrary to deep-rooted values, they feel internally conflicted.

Reasons for Conflict

Individuals become involved in conflicts when beliefs, goals, and interests clash or when needs are not met. According to Tim Ursiny, a counselor who works as a success coach and author of *The Coward's Guide to Conflict: Empowering Solutions for Those Who Would Rather Run Than Fight*, people most often experience conflict over differences in perspective (the way we see situations) and differences in beliefs, actions, or interests. "Sometimes these differences are verbalized and sometimes they are not," Ursiny writes, "but either way conflict exists."[1] For example,

1. You differ with someone over *perspective*: A new student in your school "steals" your best friend. You become angry with the newcomer and see her as too pushy and insensitive. As you get to know the new student, however, you are surprised to learn that she sees herself as friendly and outgoing and had no idea that you see her as an intruder.

2. Your *beliefs* differ from those of someone else: A close relative dies and someone you thought was his friend cannot attend your relative's memorial service because

of religious beliefs about attending a service in a church not of his denomination. You no longer feel friendly toward your relative's friend.

3. A clash occurs over differences in *goals and interests*: Brian and Emily, co-owners of a horse, fought over differences in personal goals and interests. Differences in goals and interests often arise over control issues. For example, both Brian and Emily believed they had the right to control who would ride the horse and when it would be ridden, and neither was willing to hand over control to the other. The horse was caught in the middle, as both Brian's and Emily's friends waited for turns to ride, and the animal acted out the nervousness he felt. Had one of the riders been hurt, the conflict might have expanded to include the parents of Brian's and Emily's guests.

Sometimes all of the above issues are present in a conflict. For example, the conflict in the Middle East that is so often in the news involves two homelands—Israel and Palestine—that have been fighting for decades. Israel was created out of Palestine in 1948 to give the Jewish people a place of their own to settle after World War II. A simplified version of the conflict is that the Palestinians have long been unhappy about giving up land for a Jewish settlement, and both nations want a section of land for their own that includes the ancient city of Jerusalem. Neither side is willing to give up more land or control of the area to the other. The conflict is further fueled by the fact that the Israelis and Palestinians have differing belief systems, since the Israelis are largely Jewish and the Palestinians are predominately Muslim. Israeli and Palestinian Christians also live in the area. No permanent solution has yet been found, and thousands of people on both sides have been wounded or have died during the years of fighting.

Types of Conflicts

Conflicts have been categorized in many different ways. Some sources type conflicts according to those involved:

1. **Intrapersonal:** A conflict felt within one's self. For example, assume you have secretly witnessed a bullying incident near school where the victim was seriously injured. You want to tell the authorities what

Brian's and Emily's dispute over their horse is an example of an interpersonal conflict.

you saw but are afraid the bully will find out and will then come after you.

2. **Interpersonal:** A conflict between or among two or more people. Your parents have recently divorced, and it was not a friendly parting. The two hostile adults cannot agree on anything, including division of belongings or custody arrangements for you and your brothers and sisters.

3. **Intragroup:** A conflict that arises when two or more members of the same group disagree. You are a member of the school chorus, and the group presents an annual performance fund-raiser. This year half the musicians want to present an evening of classical music and the other half is opposed. Instead, they want to perform popular music—primarily rock and rap.

4. **Intergroup:** A conflict that arises when two or more groups disagree. The school administration allows all extracurricular groups to present budgetary needs at an annual meeting with the student council. The groups equally divide a small amount of money provided by the school board, but this year some groups insist they need a bigger share of the pie than other groups. The meeting ends hopelessly deadlocked, with some group members insulting others. Groups that have worked together in the past are now vowing never to cooperate again.[2]

It is not uncommon for a conflict to begin as intrapersonal or interpersonal and then to include more individuals, as in the following example. The concert band is traveling on a school bus to another city for a music festival. Alicia and Brandy sit together. Justine and Clarice share the seat ahead of the two girls, and the four are talking. Alicia has previously admitted to the group of girls that she likes Troy, who plays drums in the band. Clarice also secretly likes Troy (this is the intrapersonal conflict), and she chooses a quiet moment on the bus to remark loudly, "Hey, everyone, Alicia likes Troy." (Now the conflict has become interpersonal.) Troy, who is sitting in the back of the bus, blushes as the boys sitting next to him tease him. Alicia is mortified and shouts, "Clarice, shut up and mind your own business." Brandy immediately takes Alicia's side: "Geez, Clarice, that was not cool." Justine likes Clarice, and she sides with her. Soon the other band members on the bus are choosing sides. The conflict between Alicia and Clarice has escalated to include other band members (an intragroup conflict). Both girls are embarrassed, and by the end of the day, Clarice considers quitting band.

Another way of categorizing conflicts is by the source of the conflict:

1. **Relationship Conflicts.** Relationship conflicts occur between or among individuals with strong ties, as in families, close friendships, or romantic relationships. When strong negative emotions (for example, anger, jealousy, or resentment), misperceptions, stereotypes, poor communication, or negative behaviors intrude on a close relationship, conflict often results. For example, if an adult family member seeks a romantic relationship outside of the marriage or if a child becomes addicted to drugs, the affected family is headed for conflict.

2. **Data Conflicts.** Data is information. Data conflicts occur when people lack the information they need to make wise decisions or when they are misinformed. For instance, assume you are taking a test in class and you believe the person next to you is looking at answers she has hidden under her hand. You report the "cheater" to the teacher, only to learn that she was not cheating at all. The person you wrongly assumed was cheating now dislikes you and seems bent on making your life miserable.

3. **Interest Conflicts.** Interest conflicts arise when there is competition for a "prize" or goal that cannot be shared. For example, James is running for president of the student council against Sharon. Both have 3.5 grade point averages and are good public speakers, friendly and outgoing, and interested in a variety of school issues. Obviously, only one student can be elected president, and a vicious, name-calling campaign battle takes place that makes James and Sharon enemies for the rest of the school year.

4. **Structural Conflicts.** Structural conflicts are caused by forces outside the control of the people who become involved. For example, a new superintendent is hired in your school district, and he and the school board extend the school day by half an hour—a decision that angers most students and several teachers. Or you have always helped your school's theater group with scenery design, but a new theater arts teacher chooses someone else to design scenery, and you are angry over his decision.

5. **Value Conflicts.** We each have strong opinions about what is good or bad, right or wrong, just or unjust. These opinions represent our values, which were formed mostly from family, religious, and cultural influences. When other people attempt to force their value systems on us (or vice versa), conflict is guaranteed. A glaring example is the war pitting the United States against Middle Eastern Islamic terrorists who reject Western culture and its influence on their lives and their countries.[3]

Elements of Conflict

Maybe you have a variety of friends who are different from you and different from each other. Your circle of friends, for example, might include a shy, quiet boy; an outgoing, loud-talking girl; a meticulous, organized person; an untidy individual; a girlfriend who practices a religion different from yours; a boyfriend whose parents are wealthy and provide luxuries you do not have; a girlfriend who comes from a large family in which money is tight; and so on.

On the other hand, maybe you are uncomfortable with people who are different from you. One important element in conflicts is *difference.* Conflicts often involve differences in goals, needs, values, beliefs, perceptions, religion, gender (the way girls and boys are treated), age, social class, nationality, sexual orientation, and many other factors. Here are some examples of how differences can cause conflict.

You assume that all members of certain groups who believe or act differently than you do have nothing in common with you and, therefore, you dislike or distrust them based solely on this wrong assumption. For example, maybe students from the Middle East enroll in your school, and you assume that they all hate Americans, so you make no attempt to get acquainted or to include them in your group of friends. Similarly, have you ever avoided someone you did not know well because he or she seemed "stuck up"? Perhaps you discovered later, after you got to know this person better, that he or she was not stuck up at all but was simply shy. People often make wrong assumptions about "different" individuals or groups before they know the person or the situation.

In addition to differences, other elements that contribute to conflicts include but are not limited to the following:

Disagreements. When you express your opinion or preferences and they disagree with someone else's opinions or preferences, conflict may result. The presidential election of 2004, for example, was an occasion for voters on Republican (candidate President George W. Bush) and Democratic (candidate Senator John Kerry) sides to air their differences. Some disagreements were more heated than others, but conflict was

Conflicts can involve differences in nationality or ethnic background. People often make erroneous assumptions about others who are different from them in some way.

definitely part of the process—resolved, for the most part, by election results, but ongoing in many individuals who wound up on the "losing" side of the vote.

Problems are another element involved in conflict because differences and disagreements can cause problems. Everyone's daily life involves problems that may or may not be resolved. When problems are ongoing and difficult to resolve, it often helps for the involved parties to discuss the matter with counselors or experts in conflict resolution, which is discussed in detail below and in following chapters.

Unresolved problems often lead to disputes, where parties have recognized that there is a problem, and at least one party wants to resolve the problem.

A dispute escalates to a conflict when parties on both sides want to win.

Unfortunately, unresolved conflicts where both parties are determined to win can lead to violence, as winning at any cost becomes the goal. The violence can be psychological, emotional, and/or physical.[4]

The Value of Conflict

Any conflict resulting in violence is destructive. This includes conflicts where wars are fought, where physical fighting results, or where people who disagree with prevailing thought are punished or ostracized.

On the other hand, conflicts that are managed well can have positive outcomes. In *Reducing School Violence Through Conflict Resolution,* authors David W. Johnson and Roger T. Johnson list the following benefits for students who are able to constructively manage conflicts:

- They experience improved achievement, reasoning, and problem solving.

- They become more mature.

- They are better able to understand another person's point of view.

- They learn about themselves—what makes them angry, what frightens them, and what is important to them.

- They are more self-confident, so they become more cooperative and involved.

- Their psychological health is improved.

- They learn self-reliance and self-discipline.

- They are better able to handle stress and adversity.[5]

"Conflicts make us aware of problems that need to be solved," Johnson and Johnson add. "Recognizing that a problem exists, who is involved, and how we can solve it helps reduce the irritations of relating to others."[6]

What Is Conflict Resolution?

To resolve a conflict means to settle a disagreement with another person or group or within one's self. Conflict resolution refers to a set of techniques used to reach a satisfactory agreement between or among opposing parties when a conflict exists. There are many options for conflict resolution. You can run away from a conflict, intimidate your opponent with violence, talk the problem out with your opponent, request that a neutral third party hear both sides of the argument, or even, in some situations, file a lawsuit.

When opponents in a conflict try to solve the problem without going to court, the process is called alternative dispute resolution, a term used in Title 9 of the U.S. Code that establishes federal law for supporting alternatives to filing a court suit. Mediation and arbitration are alternative dispute resolution methods that can, in some cases, be used instead of settling civil cases in court. (Civil cases are those in which one party sues another; they do not involve crimes.) The court often orders the losing party in a civil suit to pay a certain amount of money to the winning party. Criminal cases involve crimes against the state and are not resolved by arbitration or mediation.

Mediation and arbitration both involve a neutral third party who is especially trained in alternative dispute resolution. Mediators and arbitrators may or may not be attorneys.

Mediators and arbitrators gather information, define the issues for people in conflict, and help the involved parties develop options for solving the problems that caused the conflict in the first place. After a solution is agreed upon, mediators and arbitrators help the parties devise an agreement that both will sign. The difference between mediators and arbitrators is that mediators have no decision-making powers but arbitrators do. Arbitrators issue a decision that is binding on both parties involved in the dispute. Some states require that certain types of disagreements be arbitrated—for example, some types of credit card disputes and medical complaints—instead of litigated in court.

History of Conflict Resolution

Conflict resolution is a general term used to describe a process that has been around for centuries. Histories of China, Japan, and some African countries tell of villages using peer mediation to solve disputes among residents long before formal conflict resolution methods were used in the United States. In fact, mediation has proved so effective throughout history that it continues to be an accepted method of peacefully resolving conflicts.

About thirty years ago, school administrators saw the value in teaching students to resolve conflicts peacefully, and school-based programs were developed. Currently some schools teach conflict resolution to all students as part of the curriculum, while others train specially selected students as peer mediators who can help fellow students resolve conflicts. National peer mediation programs for schools include the following:

- Teaching Students to Be Peacemakers, which was developed by David Johnson and other researchers in the mid-1960s at the University of Minnesota.

- The Children's Creative Response to Conflict program, which was developed in 1972 by Quaker teachers in New York City and became incorporated as Creative Response to Conflict in 1992. The program helps students, teachers, and parents learn peaceful ways to successfully resolve conflicts.

- Educators for Social Responsibility, which was founded in the early 1980s and addresses violence in schools through the Resolving Conflict Creatively Program, developed in 1993 and now offered in 375 schools nationwide.

- Operation Respect, which is one of the most recent national conflict resolution programs. It was started in 2000 by folksinger Peter Yarrow, a member of the 1960s folksinging trio Peter, Paul and Mary. The program uses music to bring students together and teaches ways to resolve conflict through classroom activities. The program's focus is the song "Don't Laugh at Me," and the organization offers free educational resources designed to help reduce "the emotional and physical cruelty some children inflict upon each other by behaviors such as ridicule, bullying, and—in extreme cases—violence."[7]

One School's Example

Walnut Middle School in Grand Island, Nebraska, is an example of one school that started its own program to teach anger management and conflict resolution. This program has become a national example. School administrators decided to take action because they had often had to call police to break up

Peter Yarrow, shown here on the right with the other members of the trio Peter, Paul and Mary, started Operation Respect.

fights. In fact, during 1998—an especially violent year for the school—nearly 150 incidents of assault and fighting were recorded, some of which involved police action. By contrast, in 2003, after the program had been in place for four years, only 26 violent incidents were reported.[8] The school won the 2003 National Schools of Character award, given by the Character Education Partnership, an organization of groups dedicated to fostering character development in students.

Walnut's character development program incorporates:

- Bully prevention classes. Through skits, role-playing, and teacher- and counselor-led class discussions, students in grades six through eight are taught that bullies are weak, not strong. Bystanders to bullying incidents are asked to intervene, and students are asked to report such incidents to teachers so that bullies learn that others will not tolerate their behavior. Students also learn that verbal harassment and sexual harassment are not acceptable behaviors and that sexual harassment is illegal.

- Anger management. Students identified as bullies and those who are the targets of bullies join support groups that meet to discuss self-awareness issues.

- The Purple Hands Pledge. As part of a national campaign, students recite a pledge at the beginning of each school day: "I will not use my hands or my words for hurting myself or others!"

While the Walnut School program is not specifically labeled "conflict resolution," it has helped achieve the same goal—peaceful problem solving—as peer mediation and other conflict resolution programs for students in schools nationwide.[9]

Historical records worldwide are full of examples of conflicts that were resolved through courage, perseverance, and peaceful objection to the status quo. Here are a few examples of large-scale conflicts that resulted in positive change:

- The debate between the Federalists and anti-Federalists in eighteenth-century America that led to the Bill of Rights.

- Mohandas Gandhi's peaceful opposition to the British government's discriminatory treatment of people in Africa and India that led to independence for India in 1947.

- Martin Luther King's nonviolent persistence in demanding equal civil rights for African Americans in the United States that led to the Civil Rights Act of 1964.

- The successful negotiation, over a period of two years—1985 to 1987—between President Ronald Reagan and the U.S.S.R's General Secretary Mikhail Gorbachev of a mutual nuclear arms reduction treaty.

- The ongoing efforts of former U.S. president Jimmy Carter (1977–1981) to promote freedom, democracy, and human rights around the world that won him the Nobel Peace Prize in 2002. Among his well-known efforts to promote peace are the Camp David Accords, which were history-making agreements signed by Egyptian President Anwar Sadat and Israeli Prime Minister Menachem Begin in 1978. (Camp David is the presidential retreat located in Frederick County, Maryland, near Washington, D.C.) Carter had long wanted to help bring peace to the Middle East, and the Camp David Accords were noteworthy for getting the Egyptian and Israeli leaders to sit down together to talk. Unfortunately, the accords did not lead to a lasting peace between Palestine and Israel.

The Value of Conflict Resolution

There are many types of and reasons for conflict, but, fortunately, there are also ways to resolve conflict without fighting, making enemies, or feeling that you are always giving in to others. Compromise, negotiation, and collaboration are methods of conflict resolution that determine the needs of all individuals involved in a dispute and work to satisfy those needs peacefully. To resolve conflicts satisfactorily, the parties involved need to be skillful listeners and truthful communicators. These skills can be learned, and they are discussed in more detail in following chapters.

Some people come naturally to conflict resolution because they were raised in an environment where resolving conflicts by talking with and listening to others was the norm. Others may have been raised in environments where conflicts were never truly resolved but were temporarily handled by aggression, force, running away, or by simply ignoring the problem. Whatever your background or present methods of handling conflict, this book will help you to do the following:

1. Think differently about conflict. Instead of seeing conflict as a fight with someone, with one side winning and the other losing, you can learn to see it as a challenge that can be creatively resolved so that everyone involved feels that he or she has won something and that this is a win-win situation that leaves all parties satisfied.

2. Learn that no matter how hopelessly deadlocked a conflict seems, there are ways to settle it peacefully and satisfactorily.

3. Explore the many ways of resolving conflict so that you are aware of options open to you when you experience conflict.

4. Become a person who automatically thinks of ways to resolve conflicts with dignity and integrity so that none of the individuals involved feels like a loser.

5. Learn how to practice conflict resolution when you need to so that conflicts don't get you down and destroy relationships you value.[10]

Conflict resolution skills will not only help you preserve relationships, they will also earn you the respect of others and ensure that you can successfully settle a disagreement while maintaining your self-respect and peace of mind.

Every day of your life, as long as you interact with others, you will face conflicts.

- Getting up early to go to school may be a conflict because going to bed at a reasonable hour at night is also a conflict.

- Maybe your boss wants you to work an hour longer at your part-time job, instead of quitting at your usual time. You don't want to, but you don't have a good excuse not to, and you don't want to risk offending your boss and possibly losing your job.

- Suppose a good friend is having a party and you really want to go. However, you and your dad have tickets to a football game that same night, so you will have to make a difficult choice. If you skip the party, you are afraid your friend will be mad at you, but if you turn down the football game, your father will be disappointed.

- Perhaps you are a member of your school's student council and a motion is made that you don't like, but your arguments go unheard and the motion passes.

- A girl you consider a close friend does not answer when you speak to her in the hallway between classes.

And on and on . . .

Whether or not you realize it, you are experienced at handling conflict. If you're not always satisfied with the way you've handled conflicts, however, you can learn how to improve your conflict resolution skills. Conflicts in your life that have been the most worrisome probably share one or more of the following characteristics:

- A disagreement makes you really mad at a parent, brother or sister, friend, teacher, or someone else.

- You have difficulty going about your daily business because of a disagreement that you have been unable to settle. You cannot eat or sleep, you have become irritable, and your schoolwork is suffering. (Bullying often causes these reactions in victims and is discussed in chapter 3, "Why Resolve Conflicts?")

- You have been trying to ignore someone who is harassing you, but it isn't working. Your harasser has constantly teased, berated, and challenged you, and you want it to stop.

- You disagree with an adult authority—a teacher, your boss, your parents—over an issue that is important to you. You feel powerless to change the situation, and you fume in silence.

- You realize that making a decision entirely on your own will not successfully resolve a problem. You need to involve the individuals on the other side to remedy the situation.

Methods of Resolving Conflict

Once you determine that you have a conflict with others that requires more than a quick decision to settle, you can decide how to handle the situation. The method you use to resolve a conflict will probably depend on your goals and how much you value your relationship with the other party. There are several ways, some more constructive than others, to resolve a conflict without resorting to aggression or violence. The best ways to resolve conflicts are usually win-win in nature. That is, they let both sides win something. Here are five basic ways of resolving conflict.[1]

1. Avoidance or denial. Walking away from a conflict may be an option if one or more of the following conditions exist:

   - No relationship exists between you and the person with whom you are in conflict.

   - There is a relationship, but it is not important to you to continue it.

   - The conflict is not important to you.

   - The conflict bothers you, but the timing is wrong for a confrontation, and you need a cooling-off period.

   If you can walk away from the conflict without feeling bad, you can consider the conflict resolved, at least from your viewpoint. For example: A large group of striking employees is picketing in front of a store you want to enter. The strikers are aggressive and insist on blocking your way. A classmate of yours is one of the strikers, and he zeroes in on you. You can postpone shopping in that store, or you can go to another store that sells the same products. Since you do not know the striking classmate well, you decide to avoid confronting the strikers and you leave.

Denial is also a form of avoiding conflict. Denying that the conflict exists is not generally an acceptable resolution because it results in a win-lose situation, and chances are the issue will not disappear but will build. If you simply deny to yourself that a conflict exists, you will probably continue to feel resentment and anger. For example, when Rebecca's family built a backyard pool, she invited Susan, her best friend, to swim nearly every afternoon after school while the weather was warm. Others soon heard about the pool, however, and Rebecca did not know how to limit swimming guests. Several rowdy boys and girls started showing up to swim. After a few days, Susan was no longer enjoying herself, so she quit going to Rebecca's house to swim. Rebecca was unhappy with the situation but had no idea how to solve the problem, so she simply denied to herself that it existed. During the next few days, she seldom saw Susan after school, and she was mad at her friend for ignoring her. When Rebecca's mother asked why she seldom saw Susan anymore, Rebecca snapped, "I don't want to talk about it. Leave me alone," and stomped off to her room.

2. Accommodation. Giving in to the demands of others is fine if this is your decision and you are happy with the outcome. Some conflict resolution experts call this suppression or smoothing over, however, which is generally not a good way to resolve conflicts because it results in a win-lose outcome and can lead to resentment. In the following example, Charlett accommodates her great-aunt without feeling resentment.

Charlett's ninety-year-old great-aunt invited the family for brunch every other Sunday. Since her great-aunt believed that girls should wear dresses for special occasions, she would be disappointed and possibly angry if Charlett were to wear slacks or jeans. However, Charlett often left her great-aunt's house to join her friends for a bike ride or some other activity, and dressing up for brunch meant that she had to take a change of clothes. It was inconvenient, but rather than oppose her great-aunt, Charlett took another set of clothes to wear when she left her great-aunt's house. This was an accommodation that Charlett agreed to make to spare her great-aunt's feelings.

Accommodation is no solution, however, if you do not want to give in to the demands of others or if giving in can have serious emotional or even physical consequences for you. For example, Jeffrey developed asthma early in his life, and by the time he was fifteen, his doctor had identified several substances that caused him to have asthma attacks. One such trigger was animal dander. Jeffrey's friends knew about his asthma but had never witnessed one of his asthma attacks. When one of the boys who lived on a ranch invited the group to go horseback riding, they talked Jeffrey into going. "Don't be such a sissy," they chided. "So you'll cough a little for a while. It will be worth it." Jeffrey let himself be persuaded, and as a result he suffered a serious asthma attack and had to be rushed to a hospital.

3. Power or dominance. If the parties involved in a conflict agree to settle the matter by majority rule or agree to let a person in authority solve the problem, the conflict is resolved. This method of settling a conflict can work if involved parties see it as fair and have agreed in

advance to use the method. It is also acceptable if the authority who will make the decision is respected and trusted. Disadvantages, however, are that a win-lose situation has been created and that "losers" may feel ignored or disrespected.

A mediator may be a trusted adult when teenagers or younger children are involved in a conflict, or he or she may be a student trained in peer mediation. In schools that have a peer mediation pro- gram, trained student mediators may be asked to help resolve a conflict that seems hopelessly deadlocked. Peer mediation is discussed in detail in

Denying that a conflict exists is not generally an acceptable resolution because it results in a win-lose situation, and chances are the issue will not disappear but will build.

chapter 5. In the following example, two students allow a mediator to solve a conflict that grew until it was out of control.

Natalie and Barbara had been best friends in mid- dle school, but when the two girls entered high school their relationship changed. Natalie was more outgoing than Barbara, and she won a spot on the cheerleading squad. Barbara had always wanted to be a cheerleader but was too shy to try out. After Natalie became a cheerleader, Barbara was jealous, but instead of voicing her concerns to Natalie, she avoided her former friend. Barbara stewed in silence until she had convinced her- self that Natalie was a snob. To retaliate, Barbara told another cheerleader that she thought Natalie was tak- ing drugs. The rumor soon spread. Natalie heard that Barbara had started the rumor and she confronted her former friend. Barbara denied that she had spread the story and accused Natalie of being "too stuck up for former friends" after she became a cheerleader. A teacher heard the girls arguing and suggested they request peer mediation to resolve their differences. Neither girl wanted to bring in a third person, but the teacher convinced them to try mediation. A peer mediator worked with the girls and, while the friendship was not restored to its former closeness, Barbara agreed not to spread any more vicious rumors about Natalie, and Natalie agreed to include Barbara in some of the activities they had shared before Natalie became a cheerleader. (A 2002 survey for the Colorado Trust and Families and Work Institute found that two thirds of young people have been teased or gossiped about in a mean way at least once in the past month and one fourth have had this experience five times or more.[2])

4. Compromise or negotiation. Compromise and negotiation are useful when resources are limited (as in the example of one horse for Brian and Emily to share). This is often the most satisfactory way to resolve a dispute but only if both sides trust and respect each other, have enough leeway to give, and realize that they probably will not get everything they want. Compromise implies that each side in a conflict will have to give up something they want so that both sides can come away at least partially satisfied. Some goals on each side of the conflict and some part of a relationship may have to be sacrificed to reach a compromise, but it is still a win-win method of resolving a conflict.

In the chapter 1 conflict over sharing a horse, Brian and Emily decided on a compromise where Emily and her friends would have sole use of the horse on Saturdays, and Brian and his friends could ride on Sundays. During the week, the co-owners could each

Anwar Sadat of Egypt, Jimmy Carter of the United States, and Menachem Begin of Israel celebrate the Camp David Accords with a historic handshake. Agreements between governments often involve compromise.

ride for one hour, but only after homework and chores were done. If either sibling violated the agreement, that person would forfeit all riding privileges for one week. Since the compromise involved limiting riding time for both Brian and Emily, neither got what he or she really wanted—complete control over the horse without limitation—but both sides could ride during their specified times without interference. The compromise the two negotiated resolved the conflict, but neither Brian nor Emily got what he or she really wanted—freedom to ride whenever he or she chose.

5. Collaboration. Collaboration is a method of conflict
resolution that works well when more than two individuals are involved. When members of a group are
in conflict with each other but agree on a mutually
satisfying resolution, this is collaboration. As in a
compromise between two individuals, all parties seldom get everything they want.

As a member of his school's student council, Steven
often collaborates with other council representatives to
recommend changes to the school administration that
students believe will benefit the school. For instance,
when a student in Tennessee started a movement to
get students to sign wallet-sized pledge cards that they
would stop taunting others and would encourage
kindness, Steven lobbied his student council members
to also adopt the pledge. Some council members
thought the pledges would be simply symbolic and
therefore ineffective, since there were no enforcement
provisions or methods of measuring success. Steven
persisted in requesting that students in his school be
offered the chance to sign the pledges, and the student
council finally agreed to bring the suggestion to school
administrators. The administrators liked Steven's idea,
and six months after a majority of students had signed
the pledges, Steven noticed a difference in his school.
"People are nicer to each other," he remarked, "and
some kids who had been picked on aren't any more."

Violent responses to conflicts are, of course, always
undesirable. These responses include shouting, name-
calling, and physical fighting. Less violent but still
undesirable responses include rolling the eyes, arguing,
being overly critical and unfair, or harassing other
individuals involved in the dispute.

Getting What You Want

In *Getting What You Want: How to Reach Agreement and Resolve Conflict Every Time*, author Kare Anderson emphasizes that the answer to resolving conflict is not to change other people or to show them up as wrong. When the situation heats up, Anderson recommends, use the following four steps to keep resolution on track:

1. Remind yourself that in most conflicts, there are no good and bad guys. Those involved in the conflict may be irritating to each other, but neither side is absolutely right or absolutely wrong.

2. Remember that you may have to take it upon yourself to lower your voice, cool down, and deal rationally with the situation. If you wait for the other side to calm things down, it may never happen.

3. If you feel yourself getting more and more angry, ask yourself why you are reacting so strongly so you can let go.

4. Ask yourself how (or if) the differences between you and the other side can be fixed.[3]

Sometimes controlling a conflict situation means defusing another person's anger, says Gary Harper in *The Joy of Conflict Resolution*. Because anger overrules reason, it is hard to solve any problem when one or both parties are mad. To get started discussing a problem with a person who is shouting, name-calling, stomping around, and otherwise showing anger, try these basic tools:

- Give the person a minute to storm without interrupting, then say something like this: "O.K., now tell me that again without swearing."

- Create speed bumps. As a person's anger builds, he or she may be incapable of listening for long, but if you simply

Letting the other person express anger for a few minutes without interrupting them can help defuse the situation.

say the person's name or repeat a key word or two, you may slow the momentum and help the person's anger spiral down.

- Show empathy. When you can get a word in, tell the person that you are trying to understand. "I know how you feel," is sometimes just a red flag that encourages an angry person to tell us no, we do not know how she feels. But if you can let the person know that you are truly listening, maybe she will begin to calm down. For example, you might say, "I can see that this has really ticked you off" or "sounds as though you think you're being blamed here."[4]

The above techniques for defusing anger are part of active listening, which is discussed further in chapter 4, "Solving a Problem."

Although you are not always in complete control of a conflict situation, you are in control of your own behavior. Anderson tells the tale of a man who had bought his morning paper at the same newsstand for many years. The proprietor of the newsstand was always grumpy and unfriendly, but the man continued to say a cheery, "Good morning, Sam," every day and to ignore Sam's snarling response. A person who observed this behavior asked the man why he continued to be nice to Sam when he was so unfriendly. The man replied, "Why should I let someone else determine my behavior?"[5]

If you have ever been involved in a conflict that seemed to go on forever and that left you sad, angry, and resentful, you know how important it is to learn skills that will help you satisfactorily settle a dispute. Even if you have never experienced the anxiety a hostile conflict can cause, learning conflict resolution skills can help you through life's everyday conflicts.

3 Why Resolve Conflicts?

When conflicts are not resolved and hostility simmers, at best relationships can be destroyed and peace of mind shattered. At worst, emotional and psychological damage can result, and physical violence can erupt.

Recognizing Conflicts in the Making

You may think a conflict with someone else is easy to spot, that heated arguments will be the first clue that something is wrong. That is not always the case, however. Remember when a friend did not speak to you for a week and you had no idea why? Or a person quit dating you when you thought the two of you hit it off well? Or when you realized that you no longer had much in common with a longtime friend and the friendship was slipping away? A conflict would not exist in the above situations if no one involved was bothered. The first clue that a conflict exists is when one or both parties is unhappy with a situation and wants it to change. When you know you do not want a situation to continue as it is, it may be time to think about ways to define and resolve the conflict.

What if you want to change a situation and other parties involved seem to think everything is just fine? In that case, consider the following options:

- Ask the other person to meet with you privately.

- In a nonthreatening manner, ask the person if there is a problem. If his or her answer is no, tell the person that you think there is a problem and explain why.

- As you discuss the situation, practice creative listening and ask for feedback. Do not make accusations.

- Try to listen to the other person with an open mind.

- Don't blame the other person.

- Try to work out a compromise that satisfies both of you.[1]

Similarly, sometimes inner conflicts sneak up on us unannounced, like that time you so wanted to be part of a certain group that you shoplifted some gum just to prove you were cool. (Then felt so conflicted you decided the stunt wasn't worth the guilt trip.) You need to get your homework done, but the TV keeps distracting you. You know you should exercise, but it is too easy to be a couch potato. Inner conflicts are with us all the time, and when neglected or allowed to pile up, sometimes they become a more serious problem—called neurosis—a condition that requires professional help and is beyond the scope of this book.

Conflict cannot always be avoided, but if you can recognize certain signs that a conflict is brewing, you may be able to head it off or at least reduce the impact. For example, what are your personal triggers? Are there words or behaviors that always set you off? Maybe your personal triggers are certain facial expressions, a tone of voice, a pointing finger, or a specific phrase. For example, "you always . . ." was a phrase that, for Marge, could turn a minor argument into a fight. "You always make me wait; you always turn things around; you always . . ." No one "always" does anything, Marge believed, and when someone told her she "always" did something irritating, she felt like fighting. You usually can't stop others from raising your irritation meter in the first place, but if you feel your temper rising in response to a trigger, you might walk away, count to ten before responding to give yourself time to cool off, ignore the remark or behavior (hard to do), or—and this choice is doubly hard—if you know the statement is true, you might apologize. For example, if a friend is irritated with you because, she says, "You always make me wait for you," and you know you do tend to run late, you might apologize, but you might also want to make a stronger effort to be on time. The point is, once you recognize your personal triggers, you can better control your emotions, which can lead, in turn, to heading off or resolving a conflict.[2]

> Conflict cannot always be avoided, but if you can recognize certain signs that a conflict is brewing, you may be able to head it off or at least reduce the impact.

Another method that often prevents a conflict or defuses a brewing conflict is actively listening to others. Trying to get a point across to someone who is not listening is like talking to a wall. It is also discouraging and maddening. You don't like it, and neither does anyone else. On the other hand, active listening shows others you care about what they have to say. Here is how it is done:

1. Make eye contact when someone talks to you. Don't look off into the distance, examine your shoes, or look over the speaker's head. Show your interest by focusing your attention on the person talking to you.

2. Use body language to show your interest in the speaker. That is, don't sit or stand stiffly with your arms crossed tightly over your chest; don't tap your foot and act impatient; and don't frown fiercely, roll your eyes, or otherwise act disinterested or disrespectful.

3. Try your best not to interrupt. When someone interrupts you, it makes you feel as though you didn't get a chance to finish your thoughts and that they aren't important to the other person.

4. Don't listen like a fence post. Nod your head, or make an occasional positive comment. "What happened next?" "Tell me more about that."

5. Give feedback to the speaker to be sure you understand, but feedback shouldn't be corny or foolish, as in "Hmmmm, you don't say." Instead, try to get the person to say more. For example, if your friend says, "I hate English class," you might simply ask why. It could be your friend's underlying feeling is not that English class stinks but that her teacher isn't grading fairly or that someone in class is picking on her. The fact that you are genuinely listening can help, just as someone who actively listens to you can often help you avoid or resolve a conflict.[3]

As in anything else worth doing, active listening takes practice. Try practicing it the next time someone wants to talk to you and you may find that what goes around comes around—because you have actively listened to someone else, they will truly listen to you.

Bullying

Bullying is a type of conflict that is often difficult to resolve because the victim wants it to stop, but the bullies feel powerful in controlling someone who is weaker or different from them, and they do not usually want to change the situation. Bullying involves calling people names, saying or writing nasty things about them, leaving them out of activities, not talking to them, threatening them, or making them feel scared, anxious, or embarrassed.

People bully for several reasons. Sometimes it makes them feel popular or important. Or they may feel jealous of the people they bully or inferior to them, and they do it to "even the score." Bullies also enjoy the sense of power and control they get when they pick on someone else. In some cases, bullies do not even realize that their behavior is hurtful. (Or they refuse to admit it.) Whatever the reasons, bullying is wrong and creates serious external and internal conflicts for victims that should not go unnoticed or unresolved.

People who are victims of bullies are usually different from the group. They might be more attractive, smarter, shorter, taller, have nicer clothes, be of a different race, or simply seem too weak or frightened to fight back.

Bullying is harmful because it makes victims feel bad about themselves and hate going to school, and sometimes it even makes them physically sick. Because bullying can cause depression, victims of bullying have even committed suicide. (Suicide caused by bullying is called "bullycide.")[4]

Because bullying causes emotional and psychological harm and also often leads to physical harm, schools should not allow it to continue. Most victims of bullying cannot resolve the situation on their own and should ask for help from parents, teachers, counselors, or other trusted adults who have the power to intervene.

Bullying has become such a concern in schools that many

Bullying—physical or emotional mistreatment from someone who is more powerful than the victim—is a problem schools need to deal with.

school systems are dealing with it in special programs, assemblies, and counseling programs that emphasize bullying is hurtful. Some states have even passed antibullying laws that make bullying criminal behavior. (According to the Bully Police USA, a national organization formed to speak for the victims of bullying and to lobby for state antibullying laws, at least seventeen states have passed antibullying laws or are considering such laws.) The Bully Police USA Web site also reports that:

- Three out of every four students report that they have been bullied.

- Each month over 250,000 students report that they have been physically attacked.

- Sixty-nine percent of students believe schools respond poorly to reports of bullying.

- Studies show that both bullies and victims have problems later in life because of bullying.[5]

One Student's Experience With Bullying

Jordan, fifteen, was a victim of school bullying for three years, beginning in fourth grade, and she is now the national teen spokesperson for the Bully Police USA. In this capacity she has taped television messages about bullying and its consequences. Jordan says of her experience:

> One day I went to school and my best friend wouldn't talk to me anymore. I tried to sit by her at lunch and she picked up her stuff and moved. I tried to play with her at recess and she called me a bitch and ran away from me. Pretty soon all the other girls saw what she was doing and decided to join her, and that's when my hell started.

As the bullying increased, Jordan started chewing her nails and cracking her knuckles, losing weight, and feeling sick every morning before school.

Jordan reported the bullying to a teacher, who told the elementary school principal. When Jordan's school principal and a counselor both told her that she had to expect others to be jealous because she was pretty, had nice clothes, had two parents, and her parents earned more money than most, her mother became involved. Jordan's mother collected evidence—e-mail messages, notes, and telephone calls that threatened her daughter's life—and found witnesses to incidents of abuse at school, where Jordan was pushed, tripped, hit, spit on, and often surrounded by a group of six to eight hateful girls who told her she was too ugly to live.

The summer before Jordan was to enter the seventh grade, her mother demanded that school administrators intervene. The abuse finally ended when Jordan entered middle school, probably because the middle school principal treated bullying seriously and scheduled an assembly to inform students that such behavior would not be tolerated.

Today Jordan is homeschooled, but she has this message for bullies and their victims:

> Words sometimes leave emotional scars that can be more hurtful than physical scars. Girls are really good at justifying it and hiding [bullying] too. They are really good at making you feel like maybe you had it coming and you actually did something wrong to start it all. No one is safe from bullying. If you are fat, skinny, ugly, pretty, smart, dumb, liked by the boys or not liked by the boys, there is no logic behind the bullying. You can't prepare yourself or do anything to keep it from happening to you, except speak out and try to let people know about it and know that no one deserves this treatment, and we all have a right to go to school in peace. Don't just take it and do nothing; there are ways to stop it. Any adult at their work would sue for harassment over a lot less than many school kids are forced to go through on a daily basis. And they would win. But this is supposed to be a "normal" part of growing up for kids. If this is normal, I don't want to be![6]

Dealing With Bullies

Elizabeth Bennett is an expert on bullying (also called peer abuse) who hosts the Peer Abuse Know More Web site, visits schools to speak about bullying, and publishes a newsletter about peer abuse. She has the following suggestions for students, parents, and others for dealing with bullying:

- Document incidents of bullying. Save threatening e-mails, notes, and telephone messages left on answering machines. Keep a journal listing incidents, dates, and those involved. Whenever possible, use a video camera to record incidents in progress.

Bullying can include isolating or excluding someone, or spreading rumors about him or her.

- Bullies don't want authorities to see them in action, so if it is happening to you or if you see it happening to someone else, tell adults in school, your parents, and/or law enforcement officers.

- When all else fails, your parents may want to contact an attorney because bullies violate your rights and often commit crimes, and they can sometimes be punished by court action.

- If you know others who are victims, form a support system. Get together to talk about your experiences and perhaps talk about possible solutions. Try not to be caught alone with bullies—travel to and from school with others if you can.

- Find out if your state has an antibullying law. If bullying is against the law in your state and you have documented incidents where you were the victim of bullies, you may have a legal case against your tormentors.[7]

Anyone can contact Bennett's Web site for help with a bullying problem, and she also provides links to other Web sites about bullying. (Bennett also works with the Bully Police USA, and that Web site is another source of help.)

What About Fighting?

Bullying can lead to fighting when the victim of abuse decides to fight back. Fighting can also result when parties in conflict let tempers spiral out of control. The object of conflict resolution, obviously, is to solve problems before they reach this stage. Sometimes, however, a situation spins out of control so fast that violence erupts before anyone can stop it. Ben, Clarice, Nancy, and Ted are middle school students who are using their study period to finish writing a skit due the next period for English class. As part of the assignment, they need to tape-record the skit, and time is running short. When they go to sign out the tape recorder from the media center, Josh is using it and won't give it up. "I'm listening to a story," he tells Ben. "That's not important now," Ben replies. "We need the tape recorder *now*." "Too bad," Josh says, and Ben pushes him. Josh takes a swing at Ben, and soon the two boys are wrestling on the floor. The fight results in detention for both Ben and Josh, and Ben's group is unable to finish their English assignment on time.

Using force may seem like a good idea in the few seconds before tempers explode, but it seldom results in satisfactory problem solving. It takes patience to resolve conflicts peacefully, but results are generally helpful and lasting.

Helpful Skills for Resolving Conflicts

Resolving conflicts peacefully requires knowledge and skills that can be learned. In addition to creative listening, these skills include:

1. Communication: Talking to persons on the other side of the conflict without threatening or arguing.

2. Calm confrontation: Giving "I" messages to others. This involves telling others how you feel without accusing them. For example, instead of "You always put me down," say, "I feel put down when you . . ."

3. Controlling your behavior: Indicate that you are communicating respectfully by refraining from eye rolling, shouting, name-calling, or other threatening or disrespectful behavior.

4. Questioning: You can learn to ask pertinent questions to help pinpoint the concerns of the opposing side. For example, you might say, "You look angry at this point. Are you?"

5. Being assertive without becoming aggressive: You can speak firmly in a negotiation without shouting, name-calling, or other aggressive behavior. "I will discuss the problem further, but I can't agree to all of your demands because . . ."

6. Providing helpful feedback: Clarifying the opposition's statements helps to clearly define the goals and expectations of the individuals involved so that misunderstandings do not continue to add fuel to the conflict. "You said that you want to resolve this

When people in conflict let their tempers get out of hand, physical fights can be the result.

quickly. Does that mean today, in a week—or do we have more time than that?"

These skills are worth learning because successfully resolving conflicts preserves relationships and gives you valuable negotiating skills that you can use for a lifetime. Knowing that you can successfully resolve conflicts also leads to a sense of pride and accomplishment that fosters self-esteem.

Even if you become skillful at resolving conflicts on your own, there may be situations where those skills do not work—as in bullying. In these cases, be sure to ask for help from an adult you trust. You can still be proud that you were resourceful enough to find a way to solve a problem.

Sometimes conflicts seem so daunting it is hard to know where to begin to resolve them. Beth, a high school junior, wanted to attend college. Her grades were good in speech, English, and creative writing but not very good in math and science. Beth wanted to major in communications at a state university after high school graduation. Beth's father was a physician, however, and he was determined that Beth follow in his footsteps. Beth's mother, a nurse, also wanted her to attend medical school and told her often how wonderful it would be to have two physicians in the family.

No matter how many times Beth tried to broach the subject

of college, her parents were either too busy to listen or they lectured about the advantages of working as a physician. Beth had always been a quiet, dutiful daughter, and she could not bring herself to introduce the conflict she knew would follow when her parents learned of her intentions. Finally Beth felt she could wait no longer, and she told her parents she was not going to attend medical school. "I'm not even interested in science, and I know I would faint at the first sight of blood," she said.

"I thought this had been decided," Beth's father said. "I don't want to hear any more nonsense about your not becoming a doctor." He was clearly not listening to Beth and even threatened to withdraw financial support if she did not pursue a career in medicine.

Beth finally asked a trusted school counselor to mediate the dispute with her father. The counselor agreed and made an appointment to visit, first with Beth's mother and father, then with Beth and her parents together. After reviewing her grades in science and math courses and her SAT scores, Beth's parents agreed that the course of study leading to a degree in medicine might be especially difficult for their daughter because she had no interest in the field and little aptitude in science.

After several meetings with the school counselor, Beth's parents finally accepted the idea that their daughter would not become a physician. "As long as you get a college degree, we can live with your choice of major," Beth's parents told her.

Had Beth not told her parents how she felt, had the counselor not helped when she did tell her parents, and had her father stubbornly continued to refuse to hear Beth's argument, she might have enrolled in pre-med and been miserable. The odds were good, too, that Beth would not have succeeded in a field she felt forced to enter.

Beth and her parents were able to negotiate a solution to their conflict because several vital facts were present:

1. The relationship between Beth and her parents was important to all parties concerned.

2. Beth was concerned about her parents' interests.

3. Beth's parents were concerned about her interests, despite their attempt to force her to accept their plan.

4. Beth and her parents were striving for the same goals—that Beth should earn a college degree and be happy and successful in her chosen career.

For all of these reasons, Beth and her parents were eventually able to negotiate a solution. Beth took the first step toward negotiating a solution when she admitted to her parents that there was a problem.

Negotiating a Solution

The goal for any negotiation is for everyone to win. While it is unlikely that both sides will get everything they want, for a negotiation to be successful both sides must feel that they have won something. After two opposing sides have recognized that a conflict exists, according to Johnson and Johnson, the following six steps can help them successfully negotiate a solution:

1. Describe what each person involved in the conflict wants.

    If the two sides do not know what they want, there can be no basis for negotiation. This does not mean that you simply demand that the other person change. And it is equally unhelpful for you to keep what you want to yourself, simply withdraw, and allow the other person to have whatever he or she wants from you.

    Accurately defining what you want requires good communication skills. Use "I" statements, listen attentively, and paraphrase your opponent's statements to be sure you understand his or her exact meaning. For example: Judith's friend Grace has told everyone that

Judith cheated on her boyfriend, Stan, and went out with Thom. The rumor is untrue, Stan is accusing Judith of cheating on him, Judith is angry with Grace, and the feud between the two girls has carried over into their classes. A teacher tells them to settle their differences or be sent to the principal's office, and the two girls arrange to meet in an empty classroom after school to talk. Grace is always late. Judith finally sees her coming, but she looks as though she has all the time in the world. Now Judith is really mad, and before she and Grace can sit down she wants to start yelling at her. Instead, however, Judith remembers learning in a class that a person should use "I" statements instead of accusing someone when she is angry. So she tells Grace, "I want you to quit telling everybody that I cheated on Stan."

> **The goal for any negotiation is for everyone to win. It is unlikely that both sides will get everything they want, but both must feel that they have won something.**

As part of step number one, the person on the other side should also describe what he or she wants. For example: Grace replies, "Well, you told everyone I was jealous over you and Stan, and I was just getting even."

2. Both parties should describe how they feel. Before two sides can reach a solution, they need to understand why the problem exists, and this involves feelings. A problem would not exist if something had not triggered a strong emotion. If feelings are not brought into the open, chances are negotiation will be broken off before a solution can be found. For example: Judith tells Grace she is angry and hurt that someone she considered a friend would "go behind her back" and talk about her. Grace tells Judith that she, too, was angry and hurt when Judith told others that Grace was jealous.

3. Exchange reasons for positions. Judith tells Grace she thought she was jealous because Grace did not ask her to her birthday slumber party. Grace answered that she didn't ask Judith because she heard she wouldn't come if she did ask her.

4. Understand each other's point of view. More conversation should follow between Judith and Grace until each can see why the other behaved as she did. (They don't have to agree with the behavior—just try to see why it occurred.)

5. Create options that will benefit both parties. The two girls can suggest options to each other that might include ending the friendship, agreeing to always ask each other to birthday events, and agreeing not to spread rumors about each other that are not true.

6. Reach a wise agreement.[1] A wise agreement will take into consideration the wants and feelings of both parties and will not make one party the winner and the other the loser. It will allow both sides to win something and should not be a temporary stopgap but a long-term solution to the problem.

Reaching an agreement through negotiation is not always as easy as it sounds. Negotiations often get stuck because one or both parties don't want to give up something of value. The human resources department at the University of Wisconsin in Madison suggests the following ten strategies to consider when negotiations get stuck.

1. When stuck, talk about how that feels for awhile. You can always get back to the original issue.

2. Try reframing the issue. That is, use different words to describe your view of the conflict.

3. If the conflict seems overwhelming because so many different issues have been brought up, break it into smaller bites. This can help you get back to the basic reasons for the conflict.

4. Clarify, clarify, clarify. Keep restating what you think the other person is saying so that it is obvious you are

Negotiating a solution requires good communication skills and a willingness to look at the other person's point of view.

making an effort to understand. This can move the other side to respond positively to your efforts.

5. Stay flexible. One or both sides may be trapped by their thinking. Come up with new options for solving the problem to get everyone out of the rut that is stalling negotiations.

6. Emphasize those areas where you agree. It could be that you have been focusing only on your disagreements, and coming up with areas of agreement may be just what is needed to move negotiations forward.

7. Clarify the guidelines you are using to evaluate the conflict. For example, if you have based the discussion solely on comments that started the conflict ("He called me a liar"), try moving on to feelings that have kept the conflict going and what can be done about them.

8. Return to your ground rules. Rules for negotiation may have been lost as the discussion went on. Are you raising your voice now, when you weren't before? Is your opponent resorting to name-calling when you both agreed this was not acceptable behavior? Go over the rules again and make sure both sides are following them.

9. Take a break. Agree to stop the discussion for an hour or a day, for example, while you think of new options for a solution, or simply let your emotions wind down.

10. Before you walk away, go over all possible solutions again. Most likely you will reach some sort of agreement, but if the negotiation is still deadlocked, you may have to walk away.[2]

Here are additional tips to help you negotiate solutions to conflicts:

- Don't wait too long to tell the other side your concerns. If you stew and become angry and resentful, when you finally confront the other person you will likely vent your anger instead of calmly stating what you want.

- Don't let emotions rule. Remind yourself to remain calm, even if others are not.

- Never negotiate to win if it means the other side must lose. This breeds anger and resentment and is not a true resolution to conflict. A win-win solution works best.

- Keep an open mind. As you listen to others, perhaps you will begin to see their side so that you can negotiate a solution that leaves everyone satisfied.

- Use your sense of humor, but don't laugh at the other person if he or she seems angry or sad, and don't make fun of the other person's wants, needs, or suggested solutions. If you can laugh at yourself, however, share the joke with others involved in the conflict resolution.

- If you have some sort of solution in mind as you begin negotiating, share it. If it works, you have saved time. If the other person doesn't like it, you have lost nothing.

- Stay flexible so you can keep offering suggestions for a solution even though you don't like some of the suggested options.

- Ask open-ended questions when you are trying to understand the other's position. An answer that explains is more revealing than a yes or no.

- Don't let the discussion get off track. When it seems to have degenerated into extended arguing, stop and continue another day.

- Decide what you want as opposed to what you need. If you are negotiating with your employer for more pay, for instance, you may *want* twice what you are getting, health benefits, and a four-week paid vacation. If you know you can't possibly get all you want, decide what you *need*—perhaps to work more hours would satisfy your financial needs—and negotiate for that.

- If it becomes clear that a resolution can never be reached, you and your opponent may have to simply agree to disagree and go your separate ways.

When Conflicts Involve Values

Sometimes conflicts go beyond relationships with others in your school or home. Sometimes you see something happening in the wider world that so conflicts with your values that you feel compelled to take action. For instance, maybe you feel so strongly about child labor that you refuse to buy any products made by companies that employ children overseas. Or maybe you are so against killing animals for their fur or for any reason that you boycott fashions that use real animal fur and become a vegetarian. There is no relationship to preserve here, but your feelings and opinions are so strong that you want things to change.

In cases where your goal is change on a large scale, such nonviolent activities as marches, sit-ins, and boycotts of products are possible ways to show your concern.

Student Diplomats

When ordinary people take peaceful, thoughtful stands against injustice, social change is often the result. And these "ordinary people" are not always adults.

A few years ago, at Monroe High School in Los Angeles, California, students who felt strongly about child labor petitioned the school board to stop purchasing soccer balls produced in Pakistan. The students' argument included these facts:

- About ten thousand children, all under the age of fourteen, stitch the balls together.

- The balls are sold in the United States for about fifty dollars each, but the children who labor to make them receive sixty cents for each ball.

The Monroe High School students convinced the school board to stop buying soccer balls produced in Pakistan, and their protest continued until Nike, Adidas, Reebok, and fifty-three other soccer ball manufacturers joined with the International Labor Organization and UNICEF to sign an agreement banning child labor in the production of soccer balls.[3]

Similarly, sixteen-year-old Patricia Soto of Los Angeles participated in rallies against sweatshops and child labor and organized a boycott of GUESS products.[4]

Seventh-grader Rylie Jones wrote letters of protest to the Disney Company about workers in Haiti who were paid twenty-eight cents per hour to produce Pocahontas and Mickey Mouse shirts.[5]

Elementary school students often make a difference in their communities. In Modesto, California, in 1998, Elisa Rockwell, a fourth-grade student, read a brochure her parents had received about Nike shoes. The brochure said that Indonesian workers (some of them children) received four cents for each pair of shoes they made. In the United States, the shoes sold for about $140. Elisa asked her parents to make copies of the brochure, which she gave to her classmates during show-and-tell. Elisa's campaign was so popular that she gave speeches in other classrooms, wrote articles for the local newspaper, and formed a group called "Just Say No to Nike."[6]

In 2002, fourth and fifth graders in San Francisco helped an organization called People Organizing to Demand Environmental and Economic Rights by helping to convince the city to turn a contaminated vacant lot into a children's park. The same group of children also helped stop the eviction of several families from their homes in the area. The students visited the contaminated lot, wrote essays, and drew pictures of the park they dreamed it could become. Then they organized a demonstration of more than three hundred children to urge the city to turn the lot into a park. The city complied, and work on the park began.

The evictions were a separate issue. To protest, the students made signs and picketed a business owned by the landlord of the homes in question. Children in the families that were to be evicted wrote letters to the landlord explaining why they wanted to stay in their homes. They also presented the landlord with a tree that they said symbolized their need to put down roots. The evictions were canceled.[7]

Students around the world have organized soup kitchens for the homeless, provided blankets to street people, written letters to foreign leaders, and otherwise helped others as they advocated for social change—all because they saw conditions in the world that conflicted with their personal values.

Students who learn the skills needed for successful conflict resolution are especially prepared to share in decision-making at the neighborhood, community, state, and national levels. Indelisa Carrillo, a former fifth-grade teacher who helped the San Francisco students in their campaign to turn a vacant lot into a park, told *Children's Advocate* in 2002, a publication for the Action Alliance for Children, that it is important for children to help with decision making "at every level. They [can] assess their community, identify a problem, create a plan, and take action."[8]

Famous Advocates of Peaceful Change

Leaders who advocate for social change are often people who have become skillful at conflict resolution. Two such leaders in the twentieth century were Mahatma Mohandas K. Gandhi

(*Mahatma* is a title that means "Great Soul") and Archbishop Desmond Tutu.

Mahatma Gandhi

Mohandas Gandhi was born in Porbandar, India, on October 2, 1869, to parents of the merchant class. In 1891, he received a law degree from University College in London. He was admitted to the British bar in 1891 at the age of twenty-two. Gandhi returned to India to practice law but was largely unsuccessful until an Indian firm with interests in South Africa hired him to represent them. Upon arriving in South Africa, Gandhi found that he was treated as inferior because of his race. On trains, for example, he was required to buy the more expensive ticket for a compartment but was not allowed to ride in a compartment. Furthermore, because he was Indian, he could not vote without paying a poll tax, obtain a business license, or own land, and the South African government did not recognize marriages between Indian couples as legal.

Gandhi spent twenty years in South Africa, where he practiced passive resistance against uncooperative South African authorities and encouraged other Indians to follow him. He knew that it was important to maintain a relationship with government authorities in order to encourage negotiation. But he also realized that he had to make the authorities aware of unfair practices and the people's objection to them before the people could hope for change. He did this peacefully, as when he refused to register and be fingerprinted—a requirement that applied only to Indian immigrants in South Africa.

Gandhi was arrested and imprisoned many times for his nonviolent civil disobedience, and sometimes his wife was also arrested and jailed for her husband's acts. In 1896, Gandhi was attacked and beaten by angry whites, but he continued his campaign against racism. He had so many followers that in 1914 the Union of South Africa made some concessions:

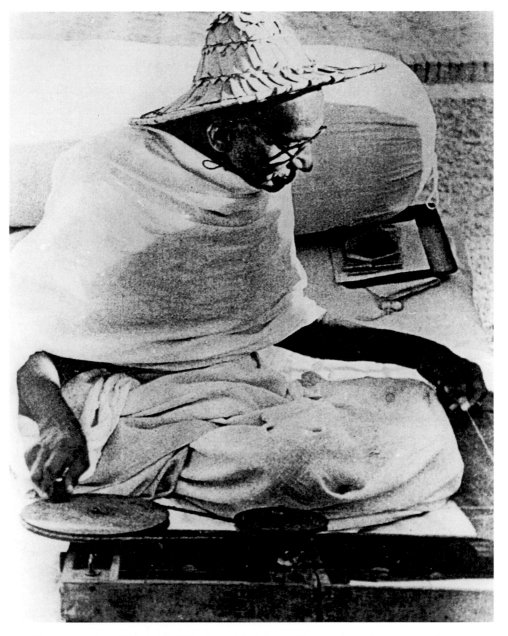

Mahatma Gandhi exemplified nonviolent resistance to the oppression of British rule in India.

Indian marriages would be legally recognized, and Indians could vote without being charged a poll tax.

Great Britain ruled India and in 1914 when Gandhi and his family returned, he and his followers campaigned for India to become independent from British rule. His philosophy of nonviolent protest was known as *satyagraha*, which means "truth force"—a combination of the Hindu words for "truth" and "holding firmly." His followers grew until they became a hindrance to business by squatting in the streets and government buildings as they demonstrated for independence from Great Britain. Britain passed the Rowlatt Acts in 1920, which gave the government greater emergency powers to deal with revolutionary acts, including nonviolent opposition. Gandhi and his followers again used passive resistance to demonstrate against the Rowlatt Acts. Frustrated British soldiers shot and killed many of the protestors. Gandhi stepped up his campaign and was arrested but quickly released.

Gandhi and his followers then effectively boycotted British goods. Gandhi hoped to see cottage industries, such as spinning, revived in India to help improve poverty among the lower classes. He became an international symbol for a free India and passive resistance. His habits of fasting, prayer, and meditation were well known by admirers. He was also known for his generous treatment of people of all races and creeds. "An eye for an eye," he once said, "only ends up making the whole world blind."[9]

In 1921, the Indian National Congress, an influential organization for Indian independence, gave Gandhi complete executive authority. Soon after, armed revolts against the British government increased. Gandhi was dismayed that people on both sides were killed, and he declared his civil disobedience movement a failure and ended it for the time being.

In 1930, Gandhi resumed civil disobedience when he began an antigovernment campaign against taxes—in particular, the salt tax. In a march that lasted twenty-four days, he led thousands of followers to the Arabian Sea, where they made salt by evaporating seawater. This was illegal, and Gandhi and sixty thousand others were arrested. Gandhi was released from prison in 1931.

Again and again Gandhi practiced passive resistance against British rule. He was jailed many times, but he never wavered from his goal of Indian independence. He fasted many times to protest violence. Finally, in 1947, partly to appease Gandhi and his many followers, the British government granted independence. Because of religious divisions, two separate states were created—India, which was mainly Hindu, and Pakistan, which was mainly Muslim. Gandhi did not want his country divided, but he finally gave in, hoping that two separate states might bring peace between the Muslims and Hindus. A Hindu fanatic named Nathuram Godse assassinated Mohandas Gandhi in 1948. History has remembered Gandhi as an international symbol of nonviolent resistance to racism and injustice.

Desmond Tutu

Archbishop Desmond Tutu is another person famous for encouraging nonviolent protest against the government in power as a means of social change. He was born in Klerksdorp, South Africa, in 1931. His father was a teacher, and his mother was a domestic worker. Tutu was raised by sympathetic and tolerant parents, and he later said of his upbringing, "I never learnt to hate."[10]

While Desmond Tutu was growing up in South Africa he lived under apartheid—a strict policy of racial segregation ordered by the all-white National Party government. Under the apartheid system, all South Africans were assigned to one of the following races: white, African, Asian, or colored. (Workers from India were classified as Asian.) Signs were erected throughout the country designating segregated areas. All races had separate housing, separate public toilets, and separate parks and beaches. Black workers could not form unions, had no representation in the government, and, like other nonwhite races, were paid much lower wages than white workers. Mixed marriages were against the law, travel was forbidden without a government-issued pass, and jobs could be categorized as white-only. Nonwhite races had separate schools that were inferior to white schools, and separate universities and colleges were also established.

During the years when apartheid was enforced in South Africa, there were many laws that discriminated against nonwhite South Africans. For example, the Suppression of Communism Act of 1950 let the government classify anyone who objected to apartheid as a communist, and that person was then subject to being banned from public meetings and holding public office and was under indefinite house arrest. The Native Administration Act of 1956 allowed the government to banish native Africans to remote areas of the country.

Despite strict segregation laws, in 1953 Desmond Tutu earned a teaching degree from Pretoria Bantu Normal College in Johannesburg, South Africa. (He had wanted to become a doctor, but his parents could not afford to send him to medical school.) He taught school in South Africa for three years but was discouraged by the poor schools for black students in his country. He decided to become an Anglican priest, resigned from teaching, and began his theological training in 1958.

Tutu was in Great Britain furthering his theological education while the antiapartheid movement was gaining momentum in South Africa. After an incident in 1960 in which sixty-nine peaceful protesters were killed by police and following the establishment of harsher laws discriminating against nonwhites, the African National Congress (ANC) abandoned peaceful protest against apartheid. The ANC, led by Nelson Mandela, formed an armed unit and battled government forces military style. As a result, in 1968, Mandela and seven other black ANC leaders

Archbishop Desmond Tutu, winner of the Nobel Peace Prize in 1984, led peaceful resistance to apartheid in South Africa.

were arrested for trying to violently overthrow the government. They received life sentences in prison.

By 1972, Desmond Tutu had finished his theology education and was in London, serving as an assistant director of the World Council of Churches. He returned to South Africa in 1975 and was appointed dean of St. Mary's Cathedral in Johannesburg, the first black to hold that position. By this time the United Nations had declared apartheid "a crime against humanity,"[11] and Tutu was gaining world attention as a spokesperson for the antiapartheid movement.

In 1978, Tutu was appointed the first black general secretary of the South African Council of Churches. He encouraged black people to use peaceful resistance to protest apartheid, and he urged the world community to stop trading with South Africa until apartheid was repealed. In response, the government canceled his passport. Ten years later, in 1988, by government order, the headquarters of the South African Council of Churches was bombed. Twenty-one people were injured.

Tutu became a spokesperson for the United Democratic Front, an organization with a membership of 3 million that was formed to protest apartheid. In 1984, Tutu received the Nobel Peace Prize, which is awarded yearly to individuals who make major contributions to world peace. The Nobel Committee recognized Tutu for "the courage and heroism shown by black South Africans in their use of peaceful methods in the struggle against apartheid."[12]

Tutu became a bishop in 1985 and an archbishop in 1986.

By 1990, economic sanctions against South Africa had begun to have an effect, and the government was beginning to see that it would have to relax apartheid rules. As part of this softer stance, Nelson Mandela was released from prison. In 1994, the all-race ANC was elected to power and the National Party became the minority party in South African government.

A new South African constitution took effect in 1996 that contained a bill of rights and ended discrimination against all minorities—including whites.

Throughout the years of apartheid, Tutu's voice was heard worldwide, condemning segregation and urging peaceful resistance to its many restrictions. Today Desmond Tutu has retired as archbishop and runs the Tutu Peace Center in Cape Town, South Africa.

Mohandas Gandhi and Archbishop Desmond Tutu put themselves in personal danger in their attempts to right society's wrongs through nonviolent opposition. No matter how often they or their followers were physically attacked, they stayed their course, practicing passive resistance in the face of racism. Most of us will never be called upon to face such opposition as we resolve conflicts in our lives. We can, however, remember their legacy of nonviolence as we deal with individuals and groups whose values and behavior are so different from our own that it seems we can never reconcile. Those are the situations where the conflict resolution techniques described in this chapter can come to our aid.

Peer Mediation

Craig, a high school junior, had an impromptu party one weekend while his parents were out of town. Carlene, a sophomore, crashed the party. Carlene's boyfriend, Josh, was there with another girl—Gloria. Carlene confronted Josh and told him she never wanted to see him again. She pushed him, making Josh angry. Josh could not hit Carlene, so he punched David, who had been trying to get the shouting couple to step outside to settle their differences. When Josh hit David, David's friend, Barry, hit Josh. Soon the party guests were taking sides in the melee, and a nervous Craig called the police. David had been hit so hard he was taken to the hospital emergency room.

The police called Craig's parents at their out-of-town hotel, and they started home.

As the result of the party-turned-brawl, Craig was grounded for a month with no television, computer, or telephone privileges. Josh faced an assault charge since David's injuries had led to an overnight stay in the hospital. Several of the boys and girls who had attended the party were still arguing at school several days later.

The above scenario is an example of an interpersonal conflict (Carlene's confrontation with Josh) that mushroomed into an intergroup conflict. Since the disgruntled parties continued to disagree and were disrupting their respective classes at school, it is also an example of a conflict that might be resolved through peer mediation.

What Is Peer Mediation?

Peer mediation is a program used in schools throughout the United States. It is a form of conflict resolution based on negotiation and mediation. Mediation implies the involvement of a nonjudgmental, objective person who helps the two opposing parties involved in a dispute settle their differences, usually when other methods have failed.

Purposes of Peer Mediation

Peer mediation programs let students within the same age group help resolve disputes between two people or small groups. In some cases, peer mediation programs may also help solve low-level discipline problems in schools. For example, students who swear at other students or start fights may be allowed to agree to peer mediation instead of being sent to the principal's office. In some schools peer mediation is used in addition to other disciplinary measures. Mediation is voluntary for everyone involved, unless offered as a choice instead of disciplinary action. Peer mediators do not make decisions to end disputes. They help the two sides in a conflict reach an agreement to avoid further trouble.

There are several reasons why peer mediation is useful, including the following:

1. It can help prevent fights, which often end in suspension from school.

> Peer mediators do not make decisions to end disputes. They help the two sides in a conflict reach an agreement to avoid further trouble.

2. It provides a forum for students, parents, teachers, and school administrators to talk when necessary.

3. It can keep hurt feelings from resulting in the loss of friends.

4. It encourages students of all ages to solve problems on their own, when possible, without help from adults.

5. It helps students learn to live peacefully with people who are different from them.

The Peer Mediation Process

Peer mediation processes vary with the schools that use them, but most programs incorporate the following features:

1. Two or more students refer themselves or are referred by teachers, counselors, or school administrators to a school's peer mediation program.

2. One or two trained student mediators are chosen to help end the dispute. (In many schools, mediators work in pairs.)

3. The mediator introduces himself or herself to those involved in the conflict, and the parties agree on the ground rules. In some programs, the disputants (those involved in a dispute) fill out pre-session forms establishing the rules. Rules generally include:

- Participants must tell the truth and must listen respectfully without interrupting.

- Participants should be committed to solving the problem.

- No shouting, name-calling, or other aggressive responses.

- Everything discussed in sessions is kept confidential unless a danger is revealed.

- Both sides must try to calmly explain the problem.

- Both sides must agree on a solution, if a plausible one is suggested.

- The parties must take responsibility for carrying out the agreement.

4. Each party is asked to describe the problem. The mediator listens to each party and writes down an agreed upon agenda that includes all the elements of the dispute.

5. Each party in the dispute tells his or her side of the story to each other. The goal is to bring out all the facts and feelings surrounding the dispute. The mediator asks questions so that the disputants can see the problem from different perspectives.

6. The mediator asks both parties to brainstorm suggestions for solving the problem. The mediator writes down all the possible solutions, indicating those that were mutually agreed upon. If no solutions are suggested, participants return to earlier steps. Sometimes additional sessions are required, or the mediator may want to meet with the parties separately.

7. The mediator writes a contract using the agreed upon solutions, and everyone signs it.

8. A follow-up session date is set so the two parties can tell how the solution is working.[1]

The Peer Mediation Process in Action

In the scenario that began this chapter, which is based on a real-life situation, a fight broke out at a party. Since emotions spilled over to the classroom, the off-campus fight became a source of disruption at school. Carlene had conducted a gossip campaign against Gloria, and Gloria had retaliated by spreading the rumor that Carlene had stolen a friend's purse. "I don't like what you've been saying about me," Carlene told Gloria in the hallway between classes. "Stop it or you'll be sorry."

"I don't know what you're talking about," Gloria responded. "And you're a fine one to talk—all the lies you've been spreading about me."

When the two girls continued their whispering campaigns against each other in math class, Mr. Thomas, the math teacher, was annoyed. He was tired of the disruption and asked the girls to stay after class. "It's apparent the two of you aren't getting along," he said. "This isn't the first time you have disrupted class. I can send you to the office, or you can request a peer mediation session." Since neither girl wanted to face the principal, both Carlene and Gloria agreed to peer mediation.

Marsha, the peer mediator chosen to help Carlene and Gloria, was not sure she could help the girls because the conflict had simmered for so long that both girls were extremely hostile. And at the beginning of the mediation process, it did seem as though finding a mutually agreeable solution would be impossible. Each girl blamed the other for the conflict. "If you hadn't stolen my boyfriend none of this would have happened," Carlene accused.

As part of the peer mediation process, the mediator writes a contract that the participants sign. The contract contains the terms that have been agreed upon.

"I didn't know he was your boyfriend when he asked me out," Gloria replied. "And you can have him, anyway. I didn't like him that well."

"And I resent your calling me a thief," Carlene countered. "I've never stolen anything in my life."

As she worked through the mediation process, however, Marsha found that there were many areas where common ground might be found. Carlene had been about to break up with Josh even before the ill-fated party because they were not getting along well. His date with Gloria gave her the excuse she needed to break off the relationship. Marsha began to realize that Carlene was actually most jealous of Gloria because of her popularity and the fact that she would undoubtedly be elected to the cheerleading squad—a dream that Carlene was too insecure to pursue.

Gloria was finally able to admit that she had made up the story about Carlene stealing and that Carlene's whispering campaign against her was more annoying than damaging.

The solution both girls accepted was that they would each stop spreading malicious rumors about each other and would work on controlling their respective tempers. A session was scheduled for the following month to assess how well the solution was working. The girls would probably never become close friends or move within the same friendship circles, but if they stopped gossiping about each other, the mediation process would have been successful.

Just as a person must constantly practice to become a good athlete, musician, artist, or public speaker, he or she must practice constantly to become a skilled mediator. Often student mediators themselves are surprised at how well the process can work. "It's amazing," Ruth Perlstein and Gloria Thrall report in their book, *Conflict Resolution Activities for Secondary Students.* "They [the disputants] seemed to be getting nowhere and we kept asking them what the problem really is and all of a sudden a light bulb went on . . . they came in ready to kill each other and walked out smiling."[2]

Here is a step-by-step breakdown of the mediation process Marsha conducted.

1. Marsha began by introducing herself to Carlene and Gloria. "My name is Marsha, and I'm here to help you resolve your conflict. I won't take sides, and I don't make decisions for you. I can't make you do anything, but I'll help you decide for yourselves how to resolve your conflict."

2. Marsha then asked the two disputants if they would agree:

   - To try to identify the problem

   - To try to solve the problem

   - Not to interrupt each other

   - Not to call each other names or put each other down

   - To tell the truth

   - To keep everything discussed in the mediation session confidential

3. Carlene and Gloria agreed to follow the session rules.

4. Marsha asked each disputant to give her version of the problem.

5. Marsha asked Carlene and Gloria to brainstorm possible solutions to the problem. (Brainstorming means to suggest ideas as fast as you think of them, without worrying if they sound stupid or unworkable. The idea is to quickly get as many suggestions as possible and sort them out later.)

6. To help the disputants arrive at the best solution, Marsha asked them to discuss the consequences of each solution.

7. Marsha asked Carlene and Gloria which solution each preferred.

8. The two disputants were asked if they thought they could keep their side of the agreement.

9. The agreement was written out, and Marsha, Carlene, and Gloria signed it.

10. Marsha asked Carlene and Gloria to come back in one month to discuss how the chosen solution was working.

Becoming a Peer Mediator

In some school peer mediation programs, the entire student body receives training in conflict resolution and peer mediation, and any student may be considered as a possible peer mediator. In other programs, students volunteer to receive mediation training, and those most qualified are accepted. The panel of adults that chooses students to participate in the peer mediation program may consist of a counselor, a teacher, an administrator, or other school personnel. Students who participate in a peer mediation program should reflect the school's diversity, including cultures, gender, behavior, academic performance, social status, and race. (Some schools claim that those students who have been labeled "troublesome" often make the best mediators.)

Students should be informed of the selection procedure, and recommendations and referrals should be considered when choosing students to train as mediators. When students choose to train as mediators, they are committing to continued skills development and willingness to conduct sessions as a team and to mentor new trainees.

Students (and adults) who are chosen to be peer mediators must receive training in conflict resolution skills. Peer mediation training usually includes role-playing, where students take the part of someone involved in a conflict and act accordingly. Most training sessions also give students a variety of problems to discuss. They try to decide what caused the problem, how the problem got out of hand, and how it might be solved. Training may also include sitting in with an experienced mediator to see how a mediation session is conducted. Training may consist of a semester-long class in conflict resolution and mediation or of workshops of varying duration.

Students who have participated in peer mediation sessions or programs agree that those who make the best mediators are:

- Trustworthy

- Good listeners

- Fair and do not take sides

- Able to maintain confidentiality

They are *not*:

- Someone who gives orders or advice

- Judgmental

- Individuals who talk about other students' conflicts

- Individuals who interrupt or focus attention on themselves

Types of Problems Peer Mediators Handle

School peer mediation programs have reported that student mediators can best handle the following types of problems: rumor and gossip, relationship difficulties, harassment, racial and cultural confrontations, classroom or extracurricular disputes, minor assaults and fighting, cheating, and vandalism. Student mediators do not handle cases that involve sexual abuse, criminal assault, theft, suicide, drug use, weapon possession, or those that involve legal problems, such as one party wanting to sue another. These types of problems require professional help from counselors, police officers, physicians, and/or attorneys.

Benefits of Peer Mediation Programs

According to peer mediation experts, research shows that students who receive conflict resolution training learn tolerance, kindness, and nonviolence, and they learn to restore relationships rather than destroy them through retribution. The positive results for schools include:

- A safer, more caring school environment

- Less classroom time spent on discipline and more time for teaching and learning

- Fewer disciplinary problems referred to the office

- Reduced suspensions, detentions, and expulsions

- A reduction in violence, vandalism, and chronic school absenteeism

Teachers, school administrators, and parents have observed the following benefits for students who participate in peer mediation sessions or are trained to be peer mediators:

- Improved communications among students, teachers, administrators, and parents

- Gaining a direct forum for resolving conflicts that does not require administrative attention or punitive disciplinary action

- An increased sense of competence, responsibility, and accountability

- Improved academic performance

- Enhanced social and coping skills

Minor fights are one of
the problems that student
mediators are trained
to handle.

Students themselves say peer mediation programs have helped them improve the following skills:

- Listening

- Communication

- Anger management and emotional self-awareness

- Critical thinking

- Problem solving

- Taking responsibility and being accountable

- Assertiveness

- Team/group collaboration

- Leadership

Sometimes despite efforts of peer mediators and disputants involved in a conflict, one or more individuals are so difficult to deal with that a conflict seems impossible to resolve. The following chapter shows how to avoid conflict or keep conflict resolution on track when certain individuals are behaving at their worst.

Dealing With Difficult People

"Sure, I'll help," Ray promised when asked to bring his pickup to help collect materials from various downtown merchants to decorate for the prom. As usual, Ray didn't show up, leaving the prom-decorating committee without enough help.

"Let's just get this done so we can get out of here," Susan, a member of the prom-decorating committee, remarked as she began throwing streamers up any old way. Typically, someone else had to come along behind Susan and correct her work.

"No, I won't help this year," Joe said, when asked to help decorate for the prom. "I worked harder than anyone last year and no one even appreciated it. I heard some kids actually criticizing the decorating theme we chose. That's the way it always goes. You work, work, work, and you're never appreciated—lucky if you even get a thank you."

Carla agreed to work on the decorating committee but criticized everyone else's work. "You can decorate that way if you want," she offered, "but I'm telling you it won't work. That tape won't hold up the streamers and everything will fall down on the dancers. But go ahead. Even though I know what I'm talking about, don't take my advice."

"You have a terrible sense of color coordination," Mel told Stephen. "You must be one of those guys who is red-green color-blind. That combination of streamers you've chosen looks sick."

"I might help later," Richard told Janice, the chairman of the prom-decorating committee, "if I can get my homework done." It was typical of Richard to say "maybe" when asked to contribute to a project, so Janice didn't count on him to show up.

Are there individuals like these in your life? Do they drive you to distraction when you have to work with them? Or (gasp) are *you* one of those people that other people dislike and avoid?

Some people change their behavior as the situation warrants. They may be happy-go-lucky and easy to get along with as long as nothing is asked of them. Or they may have certain dislikes that, if mentioned, will set them off on a tirade. Others may be so obsessed with doing a job perfectly that they never get the job done at all.

People You Can't Stand

"I can't stand him," is a common statement. We may not know why, exactly, we "can't stand" someone. We just know that we would rather not be around him or her. But what if you have to work with that person on a school project or other assignment, as in the example that opened this chapter? Then it would probably help your relationships and your peace of mind if you knew how to bring out the best in these people, or at least to tolerate them until the job is finished.

In *Dealing With People You Can't Stand: How to Bring Out the Best in People at Their Worst*, physicians Rick Brinkman and Rick Kirschner explain that most people are either task-oriented or people-oriented. Task-oriented individuals want to:

- Get the job done on time

- Get the job done right

People-oriented individuals are more concerned with:

- Having people like them as they work on a project

- Impressing their coworkers with their knowledge and expertise

When any of these four goals are thwarted, Brinkman and Kirschner assert, people can respond in ways that make others upset or wary.[1]

Several of the most common irritating personality types are portrayed in the chapter opening.

1. Ray is a "yes" person. He says yes to everyone who asks him to do something, hoping to make people like him. On the same day he promised to use his pickup to haul prom decorations, he had also promised his mother to haul used furniture to the auction barn, the football coach to haul sports equipment, and his neighbor to haul gardening tools. Typical of most "yes" people, Ray failed to keep any of his commitments. Therefore, instead of making everyone happy, as he intended, he angered everyone who had expected him to help.

2. Susan's goal was simply to get the decorating task done so she could go on to something she would rather do. She lost sight of doing the task well in her

haste to finish the job. Others were angry that they had to spend time fixing every decoration Susan hastily put up.

3. Joe's theme song is "no one appreciates me." Others are so accustomed to hearing Joe's lament that they turn a deaf ear to his complaints. Those who had worked with Joe before were actually relieved that he said no to serving on the decorating committee.

4. Carla is a "no" person. She is also a know-it-all who believes she is the only person who knows how to do a job correctly. She was willing to serve on the prom-decoration committee, but she made everyone so miserable with her constant criticizing and lecturing that they wished she had declined.

5. Mel will protest to Stephen that he "was only kidding" if Stephen gets angry over his remarks, but Mel actually seems to enjoy putting others down. His not-so-subtle personal barbs make him feel superior to others but make others feel self-conscious, put down, and angry.

6. Richard believes he has found the answer to always pleasing others. If he says "maybe" to every request for his time or services, he has not actually turned anyone down, and everyone should like him. What he has failed to realize is that when he says "maybe" then does not show up, he has taught others to distrust and possibly even to dislike him.

Other problem people can include:

• Jokers who handle every conflict by making jokes about the problem instead of discussing it seriously

• Blockers who shoot down any ideas for resolving a conflict that didn't come from them

- Hagglers who seem to want to keep the conflict alive by constantly wrangling and arguing

- Deceitful, underhanded individuals who act as though they want to resolve a conflict but sabotage any attempt to reach agreement.

These examples represent just a few of the annoying people you encounter in your daily life. The people described above are annoying but not particularly toxic. Dealing with the "yes" person, the "maybe" person, the know-it-all, the naysayer, the joker, and the critical person can be time-consuming and exasperating, but there are ways to respond to these people that can keep you from facing a conflict every time you associate with them.

1. Choose face-to-face talks over communicating through a third person. For example, instead of having your friend Kevin tell Annie that you're angry with her, tell Annie yourself what is bothering you. There is no need to put friends in the middle of a disagreement when you can just as well handle it yourself.

2. Put the person in proper perspective. Try not to take his or her behavior personally because a difficult person deals with everyone in the same manner. Be straightforward and unemotional, and be gracious and courteous even when the other person is rude. For example, you know Donna criticizes every-one, but when she tells you your skirt and blouse don't match, your first impulse is to snap, "Who made you the fashion police?" Then Donna snaps back and the two of you are angry. Instead of snapping at Donna, which would

> **Dealing with difficult people can be time-consuming and exasperating, but there are ways to respond that can keep you from facing a conflict every time you associate with them.**

probably be everyone's first impulse, try saying something like, "Thanks, Donna. That's good to know." Keep your tone pleasant and walk away. Forget Donna's remark and go about your day. Donna's probably feeling disappointed that she did not get to you, but you can smile, knowing you avoided a conflict and cut Donna off at the pass.

3. Listen patiently to the know-it-alls, naysayers, and critical people, then indicate that you have heard them and will consider their comments. Emphasize positive points and do not dwell on the negative.

4. Learn to respond to difficult people by asking questions instead of making accusations. Give and request frequent feedback. Tell the person the truth from your viewpoint: "Ray, you've said yes before and failed to follow through. We really need your help this time, so we'll be counting on you." For the "yes" person and the "maybe" person, follow up your face-to-face conversation with a telephone reminder that you need their help on such-and-such a date at such-and-such a time.

    For know-it-alls, naysayers, and critical people, you can be direct without playing their game. "I'm surprised that you think this won't work, because we have done it this way several times and it's always worked before." "We've heard your criticism, Carl. What is your suggestion for doing it a better way?" And so on. These three personality types want most of all to be noticed, and if you acknowledge their complaints and criticisms, they may eventually cooperate.

5. Don't base your goals on expecting the difficult person to change.

Toxic Personalities

According to Mike Moore, an international speaker and writer on human potential and motivation, "toxic" refers to those people who are openly or stealthily abusive and can affect you in one or more of the following ways:

- Rob you of your dignity

- Destroy your self-confidence and/or self-esteem

- Increase your stress levels

- Destroy your morale

- Make you think negative thoughts

- Decrease your productivity

- Simply make your life miserable[2]

Those types of toxic people you are most likely to have to deal with include bulldozers, volcanoes, and snipers. This type of person may also turn into one of the bullies discussed in chapter 3, and bullies are usually a more serious problem than the aggressive personalities discussed below.

1. Bulldozers are intimidating. When they approach a group or enter a room, everyone wants to dive for cover. Their only goal is to get their own way, and they do not care whom they have to push aside (or travel over) to get it. Their aggressive behavior is meant to defuse any argument before it has a chance to be heard or to intimidate those who might disagree with them into silence. Mel, who is accusing Steven of being color-blind at the beginning of this chapter, is well on his way to becoming a bulldozer.

    Bulldozers are not subtle, and they can be loud and forceful or as intensely damaging as a laser. They will often protest that their remarks or behavior are "nothing personal," even though when you are attacked by a bulldozer you feel thoroughly flattened. Bulldozers simply use any means to achieve an end. Their bad behavior may get them what they want in the short term, but it is seldom effective in the long term.

2. Volcanoes, as the term implies, are always on the verge of exploding. Like bulldozers, they are hostile and aggressive, but when they blow up they lose all control. They typically blame a problem on someone else, then blow up at the person or persons they believe caused the problem. They shout, insult, stomp around, and

Volcanoes are people who lose control, striking out and blaming those around them.

otherwise express their extreme discontent. A volcano's behavior is usually due to low self-esteem and a feeling of being threatened, but knowing this does not help the person who ends up in the middle of the volcano's explosion.

In an earlier example, Carlene was a volcano who exploded at her boyfriend for dating Gloria. Later, Carlene also behaved like a sniper.

3. Snipers don't bulldoze you or explode at you; they talk about you behind your back (as in the earlier example where Carlene spread rumors about Gloria). The sniper makes little jokes about you, criticizes your choice in clothes, and otherwise tries to embarrass you. Like Mel at the beginning of this chapter, snipers usually protest that they were "just kidding" after taking a jibe at you. They often get away with their behavior because no one wants others to believe that he or she can't take a joke.[3]

You can't change toxic people, but you can learn to deal with them. Some of the techniques for defusing another person's anger, as discussed in chapter 2, may work, and here are a few suggestions from Mike Moore's manual, *Dealing With Difficult People*, and from motivational speaker Kerry L. Johnson for dealing with bulldozers and volcanoes:

- Stand up to them—literally. Stand at eye level, or get them to sit down. Never let them stand over you while you are sitting.

- Remain calm. Your first impulse may be to respond in kind, but this often leads to physical violence. Respect the person and let him or her know that you expect respect in return. Don't settle for anything less.

- Listen attentively. Don't argue or interrupt, just listen. When the person has begun to wind down, ask him questions about his problem. Don't accuse the person of bad behavior during his tantrum. Try to draw him into a constructive discussion. This may defuse his explosion and help him to calm down.

- Look the person directly in the eye and respond assertively but without emotion or aggression. Don't accuse or judge the person; just calmly tell him how you feel. If the person interrupts you, say, "Just a moment. Please let me finish."

- If the bulldozer or volcano insists on continuing to bully you, just say, "I don't allow anyone to treat me this way." Then slowly and calmly walk away. It is also effective to calmly stare at the person during an attack, then, without a word, just turn and walk away.

- Document in writing your attempts to resolve the conflict. (This is useful if the conflict escalates to involve school authorities or if you opt for peer mediation.)

The sniper requires special handling that is different from the above tips for handling bulldozers and volcanoes. Don't respond to comments made anonymously that you hear through the grapevine, recommends Johnson. If a sniper attacks you in front of others under the guise of "joking," ignore him or her. The sniper wants you to laugh at yourself so he or she can attack again, only with more venom.

Get the sniper alone and confront him or her about comments directed against you. If he or she says, "Can't you take a joke?" say, "Sure, I can take a joke, but what you said about me sounded as though you weren't kidding. Did you mean to sound the way you did?" If the person says yes, you may discover what the real reason is behind the sniping.[4]

Handling difficult people takes skill and practice. You do not have to take all the grief they dish out; you can confront them. But remember that hostile arguments or violence are never the solution. It takes courage to confront problem people, and you cannot change them. You may, however, change the way they behave toward you.

If all else fails, you may have to separate yourself from the problem person in your life.

If you can make the above tips work for you, the difficult people in your life will no longer have control or influence over your emotions, behavior, or goals.

Do not be surprised if you have recognized your own behavior in any of the examples mentioned. We have all probably been the difficult person in the lives of others at one time or another. Maybe worries about an ill family member have made a person grumpy and uncooperative. Or perhaps a person is simply tired, and it requires too much energy to cooperate on a project. Maybe the easiest response to a request or a conflict seems to be to say and do nothing—another form of behavior that can irritate others.

There are reasons behind most disagreeable or annoying behavior, but most of us do not have the expertise to get to the source. We can only learn how to deal with the person's behavior to accomplish whatever goal is at hand or to resolve a conflict that will make life easier for all concerned.

Turning Conflict into Collaboration

Have you ever had a dream where you were trying to run from someone or something, but your legs moved in slow motion? You knew someone was gaining on you, but you felt as though you were moving underwater. That's much like the feeling of being involved in a disturbing conflict but not knowing how to resolve it satisfactorily.

You probably knew what conflicts were before you opened this book—at least you knew that you had experienced them. Now that you have reached the last chapter of the book, you have no doubt gained some insight into how conflicts develop and how to resolve conflicts so that they do not dominate your emotions, decisions, and goals. As you practice the suggestions for satisfactorily resolving conflicts, you should notice a steady increase in self-esteem and self-confidence. In addition, you should notice an improvement in those relationships that you consider important, because difficult conflicts no longer keep you on edge around certain people.

As mentioned in the last chapter, face-to-face communication is more likely to get your message across. This is true because the person you address can see your facial expressions and body language and can hear your tone of voice. For example, the comment, "So, you messed up again," is taken as the playful jibe it is meant to be if you are smiling when you say it and lightly jab the other person's arm.

On the other hand, if you scowl, raise your voice, and say, "So! You messed up again," the person to whom you are speaking will understandably deduce that you are angry.

E-mail Can Be a Source of Conflict

This is why electronic mail (e-mail), that universal method of communicating that is so pervasive in our lives, can so easily cause conflict. Since we usually think of conflicts as arising through face-to-face interaction, most of this book has discussed these types of conflicts. But e-mail messages are proving to be sources of conflict unique to the Internet Age.

No doubt when e-mail programs were written, the creators envisioned a speedy method of communication that would give computer users time for more important workplace tasks. Unfortunately, e-mail has also created a high-tech source of conflict.

"We were friends until we started e-mailing while I was out of town last summer," says Jean, a high school freshman talking about her difficulties with a former friend. "Now we hardly speak to each other."

The problem was that Tiffany, Jean's friend, sent the following e-mail message to Jean: "Don't worry, Jean, Kent [Jean's boyfriend] is having fun while you are gone." Jean took the message to mean that Kent was dating others while she was out of town, and she thought Tiffany was gloating. Jean was angry and she asked Tiffany what was going on.

Tiffany tried to explain that she meant that Kent was not having fun, but she had failed to point out that she was being sarcastic, and Jean took it at face value. Jean conjured scenarios about Tiffany stealing her boyfriend, and the friendship cooled. The moral is that it is difficult to get sarcasm or other emotions across without tone of voice and facial expressions.

> **When the person you are communicating with cannot see you or hear your voice, it is easy for your message to be misinterpreted.**

Business users of e-mail have also found it to be fast but sometimes confusing. "If you are in a hurry," says Dave, a self-employed accountant, "an e-mail message can come across as the exact opposite of what you meant." For example, he sent a message to a client to bring in additional records for income tax preparation, and the message seemed so abrupt that the client was insulted. The message read, "I need more documentation re. your business entertainment deduction a.s.a.p." The client somehow interpreted this to mean that Dave did not trust him or questioned his business deductions, and he was huffy when he delivered the requested records.

When the person you are communicating with cannot see you or hear your voice, it is easy to misinterpret the message. Here are some tips to keep your e-mail correspondence from becoming a high-tech source of conflict:

1. Reread your e-mail messages before sending them out to prevent creating unintentional conflicts.

2. Use emoticons (smiley faces) to represent your emotional state, but only in your personal e-mail to friends. Smileys are not appropriate to include in

e-mails to businesses, employers, colleges, teachers, or in other more formal situations. Most e-mail programs offer a choice of emoticons, or you can create your own using parentheses, the colon, semicolon, dash, and other punctuation marks. Some examples include:

:-) = "I'm smiling." (happy, not sad or angry)

;-) = "I'm winking." (kidding)

:-(= "I'm angry/sad."

:-o = "I'm shocked/surprised."

:-@ = "I'm screaming." (denotes outrage)

:-I = "I'm indifferent." (denotes that you don't care)

:-e = "I'm disappointed."

>:-/ = "I'm angry."

:-D = "I'm laughing."

:-$ = "Put your money where your mouth is."

:-P = "I'm sticking out my tongue."

Emoticons give the person at the receiving end of the message some idea of your state of mind so that conflicts can be avoided.

3. "Lol" after a statement or question means "laughing out loud" and can indicate that you were teasing or that you take the statement lightly and were not serious. It is annoying when overused, but when used sparingly and honestly it can also indicate that your message was intended to be taken lightly.

4. Ask for clarification of the meaning of an e-mail message you have received before you jump to the conclusion that the message is insulting or otherwise

undesirable. Ask questions such as, "Did you mean that . . . , or is this what you meant . . . ?"

E-mail has also been used as a bully's weapon, since threats can be leveled with anonymity and without face-to-face contact. Victims of cyberbullies should print copies of such poisonous messages, as proof of the abuse in case charges are brought.

Changing Your Attitude

If you find yourself constantly embroiled in difficult conflicts with others, maybe you need to ask yourself if you need to change your attitude. For example, in *Getting What You Want: How to Reach Agreement and Resolve Conflict Every Time*, author Kare Anderson asks:

1. Do you make certain assumptions about people based on certain personal characteristics, such as the way they dress? For example, "Do you assume that the new kid will be uncooperative because she's wearing a black leather skirt, spiked hair, and purple lipstick?" Anderson suggests that this person "may be the computer whiz" who can show you how to do new and amazing things on the computer.

2. Do you mark someone as unfriendly who doesn't initiate a conversation? "He may be painfully shy," Anderson advises.

3. Do you take advantage of someone who seems always cheerfully ready to help with your projects? That person, writes Anderson, "may be saying scathing things about you to half the people" you know.[1]

Anderson and other experts also warn against making assumptions about people based on certain behavior, such as:

• Smoking (They must be stupid.)

• Weird clothes (They must be clueless.)

E-mail is quick and easy, but it can be a source of miscommunication, so it's important to use it carefully.

- Putting on makeup in public (They must be airheads.)

- Dressing expensively (Their parents must be rich.)

Assumptions can lead to conflict if you slight others or otherwise treat them differently because of assumptions you have made.

Assumptions are not necessarily bad, and we all make them, Anderson writes. "They just aren't very good barometers if you really want to know and honor the truth about another person, or if you want accurate information on which to base action or negotiation."[2]

Give Yourself Positive Messages

When you speak purposefully to yourself, advise Brinkman and Kirschner in *Dealing With People You Can't Stand*, you can change your attitude toward difficult people for the better:

1. Accept the situation for what it is. That doesn't mean that you have to take abuse from someone, but if you constantly struggle with a conflict or withdraw, you will remain frustrated. When you see the situation realistically, your chances of resolving a conflict improve.

2. Try to see the conflict as an opportunity—perhaps to improve a relationship or to develop your conflict resolution skills.

3. Examine your experiences with difficult people to see what you have learned. Are you stronger because of the experience? Did you learn more about yourself from the experience? What is working in dealing with a difficult person in your life, and what is not?

4. Be flexible. Try other, novel approaches when it is clear that your methods of dealing with a difficult person are not working now and will probably never work.

5. Let conflict surface when it exists, but if you simply can't find a solution, perhaps the best attitude is, "Oh well, I can't change this person, but I can change the way I react."[3]

The tips and techniques you have learned to this point should help you resolve conflicts with others when they arise and possibly even avoid conflicts in a satisfactory manner. Two final facts to remember, however, are:

- You are not likely to change the person with whom you are in disagreement.

- Conflicts in your life will not always be resolved in your favor.

When you run up against one or both of these truths, you can let anger simmer and make you miserable, or you can tell yourself that you did everything you could do, and then move on with your life. In any event, the skills you learn for conflict resolution will help ensure that you always make the best decisions for handling conflicts wisely.

Chapter Notes

Chapter 1   What Is Conflict?

1. Tim Ursiny, Ph.D., *The Coward's Guide to Conflict: Empowering Solutions for Those Who Would Rather Run Than Fight* (Naperville, Ill.: Sourcebooks, Inc., 2003), p. xix.

2. *Understanding Conflict: Conflict Negotiation Skills for Youth*, n.d., <http://www.unescap.org/esid/hds/pub/2286/s2.pdf> (November 8, 2004).

3. *Effective Mediation Resources: Oregon Mediation*, "Types of Conflict," n.d., <http://www.internetmediator.com/medres/ pg18.cfm> (November 6, 2004).

4. *Conflict Resolution*, n.d., <http://p2001.health.org/CTW06/ mod2tr.htm#III> (November 8, 2004).

5. David W. Johnson and Roger T. Johnson, *Reducing School Violence Through Conflict Resolution* (Alexandria, Va.: Association for Supervision and Curriculum Development, 1995), pp. 16–17.

6. Ibid., p. 17.

7. "About Us," *Operation Respect: Don't Laugh at Me*, n.d., <http://www.dontlaugh.org> (January 3, 2005).

8. Sarah Schulz, "Rally For Respect," *Grand Island Independent*, October 16, 2004, <http://www.theindependent.com/stories/ 101604/new_purple16.shtml> (November 8, 2004).

9. Bob Katz, "Teaching Kids About Hurt," *NEA Today*, November 2003, p. 42.

10. Stewart Levine, *Getting to Resolution: Turning Conflict into Collaboration* (San Francisco: Berrett-Koehler Publishers, Inc., 1998), pp. xii–xiii.

Chapter 2   When Conflicts Arise

1. *Five Basic Methods for Resolving Conflict*, n.d., <http://www. draknet.com/proteus/conflict2.htm> (November 9, 2004).

2. Center for the Prevention of School Violence, "Stats 2002: Selected School Violence Research Findings From 2002 Sources," n.d., p. 3,

no. 27, <http://www.ncdjjdp.org/cpsv/Acrobatfiles/Stats_2002.pdf> (October 29, 2003).

3. Kare Anderson, *Getting What You Want: How to Reach Agreement and Resolve Conflict Every Time* (New York: Dutton, 1993), pp. 155–156.

4. Gary Harper, *The Joy of Conflict Resolution: Transforming Victims, Villains and Heroes in the Workplace and at Home* (Gabriola Island, British Columbia, Canada: New Society Publishers, 2004), pp. 74–81.

5. Anderson, p 159.

Chapter 3 Why Resolve Conflicts?

1. "How to Resolve Conflicts Without Offending Anyone," *Women's Business Center,* 1997, <http://www.onlinewbc.gov/docs/manage/conflicts.html> (November 14, 2004).

2. "Making Peace: Tips on Managing Conflict," n.d., <http://www.gibsoncountysheriff.com/resource/resource_managing_conflict.html> (November 12, 2004).

3. "Active Listening," *Coaching Center,* n.d., <http://www.coaching center.org/alliance/lead/lead3-10.htm> (August 27, 2004).

4. "What's Bullying?" n.d., <http://www.nobully.org.nz/advicek.htm> (November 12, 2004) and "Jared's Story," n.d., <http://www.jaredstory.com/suicide.html> (November 16, 2004).

5. *Bully Police USA,* n.d., <http://www.bullypolice.org/BullyPolice USA.pdf> (November 12, 2004).

6. Author's interview with Jordan Valacich, November 12, 2004.

7. Elizabeth Bennett, "Peer Abuse Know More," n.d., <http://www.peerabuse.info> (November 13, 2004).

Chapter 4 Solving a Problem

1. David W. Johnson and Roger T. Johnson, *Reducing School Violence Through Conflict Resolution* (Alexandria, Va.: Association for Supervision and Curriculum Development, 1995), p. 52.

2. Human Resources Department, University of Wisconsin, Madison,

Wisconsin, "Manage Impasse With Calm, Patience, and Respect," n.d., <http://www.ohrd.wisc.edu/onlinetraining/resolution/step7.htm#strategies_for_managing_impasse> (February 9, 2005).

3. "Children as Activists," *Parent News,* February 1998, <http://npin.org/pnews/1998/pnew298/pnew298e.html> (November 7, 2003).

4. Ibid.

5. Ibid.

6. Erica Williams, "Elementary-School Activists Impact Their Community," *Children's Advocate,* Action Alliance for Children, March–April 2002, <http://www.4children.org/news/302gse.htm> (November 7, 2003).

7. Ibid.

8. Ibid.

9. Shalu Bhalla, ed., *Quotes of M.K. Gandhi* (New Delhi, India: UBS Publishers Distributors, 1995), p. 1.

10. The Hero File: Archbishop Desmond Mpilo Tutu, n.d., <http://www.moreorless.au.com/heroes/tutu.htm> (November 7, 2004).

11. Ibid.

12. Ibid.

Chapter 5 Peer Mediation

1. Ruth Perlstein and Gloria Thrall, *Ready-to-Use Conflict Resolution Activities for Secondary Students* (San Francisco: Jossey-Bass, 1996), pp. 117–118.

2. Ibid., p. 152.

Chapter 6 Dealing With Difficult People

1. Rick Brinkman and Rick Kirschner, *Dealing With People You Can't Stand: How to Bring Out the Best in People at Their Worst* (New York: McGraw-Hill, 2002), pp. 15–17.

2. Mike Moore, "Dealing with Difficult People," n.d., <http://www.selfgrowth.com/articles/Moore6.html> (December 11, 2003).

3. Kerry L. Johnson, Ph.D., "Coping With Problem People," n.d.,

<http://self-discipline.8m.com/coping_with_problem_people.htm>
(December 10, 2003).

4. Ibid.; and Moore.

Chapter 7 Turning Conflict into Collaboration

1. Kare Anderson, *Getting What You Want: How to Reach Agreement
and Resolve Conflict Every Time* (New York: Penguin Group, 1993),
pp. 60–61.

2. Ibid., p. 61.

3. Rick Brinkman and Rick Kirschner, *Dealing With People You Can't
Stand: How to Bring Out the Best in People at Their Worst* (New
York: McGraw-Hill, 2002), pp. 224–225.

Glossary

accommodation—Giving in to the needs and wishes of others.

arbitration—Settling a dispute through a neutral third party who has the power to make decisions that are binding to both sides.

avoidance—Solving a conflict by walking away from it.

conflict resolution—Techniques for settling a disagreement with another person, another group, or within one's self.

denial—Solving a conflict by pretending it does not exist.

intergroup—Between two or more groups.

interpersonal—Between people.

intragroup—Within a group.

intrapersonal—Within one's self.

mediation—Settling a dispute through a neutral third party who does not have the power to make binding decisions.

peer abuse—Bullying.

Further Reading

Books

Drew, Naomi. *The Kids' Guide to Working Out Conflicts: How to Keep Cool, Stay Safe, and Get Along.* Minneapolis, Minn.: Free Spirit Publishing, 2004.

Rue, Nancy N. *Everything You Need to Know About Peer Mediation.* New York: Rosen Publishing Group, 2001.

Simpson, Carolyn. *Coping Through Conflict Resolution and Peer Mediation.* New York: Rosen Publishing Group, 1998.

Ury, William L., editor. *Must We Fight? From the Battlefield to the Schoolyard, a New Perspective on Violent Conflict and Its Prevention.* San Francisco: Jossey-Bass, 2002.

Wandberg, Robert. *Conflict Resolution: Communication, Cooperation, Compromise.* Mankato, Minn.: LifeMatters, 2001.

Internet Addresses

CRInfo: Conflict Resolution Information Source
   <http://www.crinfo.org>

Kids and Conflict
   <http://www.kidsandconflict.com>

National Bully Police
   <http://www.bullypolice.org>

Index